# Evangelizing the Culture
## of Modernity

# FAITH AND CULTURES SERIES
An Orbis Series on Contextualizing Gospel and Church
General Editor: Robert J. Schreiter, C.PP.S.

The *Faith and Cultures Series* deals with questions that arise as Christian faith attempts to respond to its new global reality. For centuries Christianity and the church were identified with European cultures. Although the roots of Christian tradition lie deep in Semitic cultures and Africa, and although Asian influences on it are well documented, that original diversity was widely forgotten as the church took shape in the West.

Today, as the churches of the Americas, Asia, and Africa take their place alongside older churches of Mediterranean and North Atlantic cultures, they claim their right to express Christian faith in their own idioms, thought patterns, and cultures. To provide a forum for better understanding this situation, the Orbis *Faith and Cultures Series* publishes books that illuminate the range of questions that arise from this global challenge.

Orbis and the *Faith and Cultures Series* General Editor invite the submission of manuscripts on relevant topics.

## Also in the Series

*Faces of Jesus in Africa*, Robert J. Schreiter, C.PP.S., Editor
*Hispanic Devotional Piety*, C. Gilbert Romero
*African Theology in Its Social Context*, Bénézet Bujo
*Models of Contextual Theology,* Stephen B. Bevans
*Asian Faces of Jesus*, R. S. Sugirtharajah, Editor

FAITH AND CULTURES SERIES

# Evangelizing the Culture of Modernity

*Hervé Carrier, S.J.*

ORBIS BOOKS

**Maryknoll, New York 10545**

This book is a revision of papers previously published mainly in *Evangélisation et développement des cultures,* © Editrice Pontificia Università Gregoriana, Rome, 1990. Chapter 1 is a revision of "The Contribution of the Council to Culture," in René Latourelle, ed., *Vatican II: Assessment and Perspectives* (Mahwah, NJ: Paulist Press, 1988). Chapter 2 is based on a text presented to the International Theological Commission in preparation for the document, "Faith and Inculturation," cf. *Origins,* May 1989, pp. 800-807. Chapter 3 was given at a seminar of the bishops of Nigeria on inculturation in Jos, Nigeria, 9-19 November 1988 and was published by the Nigerian Episcopal Conference (Lagos, 1989). Chapter 4 appeared in "The Parable of Anticulture: George Orwell—1984," in F. Rosenstiel and S. G. Shoham, eds., *And He Loved Big Brother: Man, State and Society in Question* (contributions to George Orwell Colloquy, "1984: Myths and Reality," Strasbourg: Council of Europe, 1986, pp. 219-26). Chapter 5 originated in a paper entitled, "Can Scientists be Spiritual Humanists?" in *Proceedings of the International Symposium: Science, Technology and Spiritual Values, an Asian Approach to Modernization* (Tokyo: Sophia University; United Nations University, 1987, pp. 276-89). Chapter 6 appeared first as "Les biens immatériels: la science, la culture et l'art," delivered at the international conference organized by the Pontifical Council for Justice and Peace in Rome on the occasion of the centenary of the encyclical *Rerum Novarum,* May 1991. Chapter 7 was taken from an article published in *Catéchèse* (January 1989), pp. 45-53.

---

**Library of Congress Cataloging-in-Publication Data**

Carrier, Hervé, 1921-
    [Evangélisation et développement des cultures. English. Selections]
    Evangelizing the culture of modernity / Hervé Carrier.
    p. cm. — (Faith and cultures series)
    Translated from: Evangélisation et développement des cultures.
    Includes bibliographical references and index.
    Contents: The church's perception of modernity — Modernity as a culture to evangelize — Inculturation — Can we still hear a counter-cultural prophet? — Toward a new convergence of science and religion? — Christians and the modern conception of cultural rights — The new evangelization facing agnostic culture.
    ISBN 0-88344-898-X (paper)
    1. Evangelistic work—Philosophy. 2. Civilization, Modern—1950-
3. Christianity and culture. I. Title. II. Title: Modernity.
III. Series.
BV3793.C3713   1993
261—dc20
                                   93-8759
                                   CIP

# Contents

89814

# Preface

Most of the discussion of inculturation in the last two decades has been focused on cultures outside the North Atlantic region. That was understandable, since the whole inculturation discussion arose because the European and North American expressions of Christianity did not seem to be connecting adequately in much of Asia, Africa and Latin America. Those connections are still by no means complete, but there is now another kind of discussion emerging: inculturation in Europe and North America.

This new discussion has been prompted by two factors. The first is the call for a new evangelization, or a re-evangelization, of cultures once considered Christian. The emphasis here is not principally upon the conversion of individuals, but upon addressing the very cultural fabric in which so-called modern societies live. This emphasis has its origins in the Second Vatican Council's reflection on modern cultures, but was made explicit by Pope Paul VI and has become a central theme in the papacy of John Paul II.

The second factor has been the transition in which modernity now finds itself. The reconfiguration of Europe since 1989, the consolidation of global capitalism, and the emergence of what some believe is a postmodern situation have all shaken modernity's confidence in itself and its project. This is providing an entry for dialogue with modernity that was less apparent just a few years before this time.

This new discussion is ably joined by Father Hervé Carrier, S.J., whose career as a religious sociologist and now as secretary of the Pontifical Council for Culture positions him well for this enterprise. In the essays in this book, he describes and analyzes the culture of modernity, and brings to bear more than three decades of Church teaching on culture and approaches to the culture of modernity. His diagnosis of modernity is acute, and his presentation of the ecclesial reflection on modernity and its culture from Vatican II through John Paul II brings together two partners in the discussion of the future direction of humanity as we enter the third millennium. For the fate of modernity affects more than Europe and North America; it also constitutes what Carrier calls here a "superculture" which, through modern capacities for communication and travel, has a profound impact on local cultures around the planet.

Moreover, a number of students of modern societies have discerned a heightened quest for religious experience, albeit a diffuse and noninstitutional one. The utopia of progress, so clearly described in this book, no longer satisfies. What kind of form will these religious yearnings take? Without a clear sense of where modernity has been and where it finds itself now, we will be unable to answer that question. Carrier helps us find our way here.

Again and again, Carrier reminds us that we must become cultural critics if we are to be faithful Christians in our own time and place. By criticism he does not mean nay-sayers. He calls for a genuine engagement with modern cultures with ever an eye to their transformation in light of the Gospel. Such an engagement cannot be carried on by the disinterested bystander; it requires commitment and solidarity.

Modernity is at a turning point, a point that invites analysis and response. This book, both a primer on modernity and a clear exposition of conciliar and papal teaching on culture, is a welcome voice in the discussion now underway.

ROBERT J. SCHREITER, C.PP.S.

# Abbreviations

| | |
|---|---|
| AA | *Apostolicam Actuositatem*, Vatican II Decree on the Apostolate of the Laity |
| AG | *Ad Gentes*, Vatican II Decree on the Missionary Activity of the Church |
| CD | *Christus Dominus*, Vatican II Decree on the Pastoral Office of Bishops |
| DH | *Dignitatis Humanae*, Vatican II Declaration on Religious Liberty |
| GE | *Gravissimum Educationis*, Vatican II Declaration on Christian Education |
| GS | *Gaudium et Spes*, Vatican II Pastoral Constitution on the Church in the Modern World |
| IM | *Inter Mirifica*, Vatican II Decree on Social Communications |
| LG | *Lumen Gentium*, Vatican II Dogmatic Constitution on the Church |
| PC | *Perfectae Caritatis*, Vatican II Decree on the Renewal of Religious Life |
| SC | *Sacrosanctum Concilium*, Vatican II Decree Constitution on the Sacred Liturgy |
| UR | *Unitatis Redintegratio*, Vatican II Decree on Ecumenism |

# Introduction

# Evangelizing the Culture of Modernity

The main theme of this book is articulated in the words of the title: "Evangelizing the Culture of Modernity." In short, modernity should be considered as a *culture* — a culture needing to be *evangelized*. The most promising aspect of the *new evangelization* lies precisely in the Church's current awareness that culture itself is now considered the decisive locus for evangelization. What is perceived as new today is that cultures require a new type of evangelization. The Gospel of Jesus Christ cannot be announced to persons of modern sensibilities and mentalities without a methodical, reflective, and concerted effort, for today the pace of cultural change defies the traditional way of Christianizing common behavior and customs.

In the past, cultures and institutions became Christian not so much through a specific strategy as through the slow penetration of Christ's teaching into life-styles and social structures. Today, the capillary spread of Gospel values into the social fabric is blocked because of the wide gap existing between the Christian faith and the prevailing ethos of the industrialized world. Announcing Jesus Christ to modern minds calls for a profound revision of traditional methods of evangelization. This is one of the main problems that the present volume examines, beginning with the new forms of dialogue between the Church and the modern world.

Our first task will be to situate the Church within the socio-cultural context of modernization, which is an ongoing process

1

challenging our secure sense of the past. On a global scale today, all cultures have become fragile due to a crisis in values, traditions, and institutions. Cultures seem swept along by an irresistible movement, and many people are now asking what moral and spiritual force can guarantee the future of the *humanum*.

As Christians, we view cultures, like all human reality, as participating in the evangelizing dialectic of life, death, and resurrection. Cultures come alive through the amazing creativity of the human mind and the fruits of contemplation. Yet cultures are often wounded by personal and collective sin, and they need purification, conversion, and continual growth in the light of the Gospel. The power of the Incarnation and Resurrection reaches everything human, and cultures are eminently human. That is why the Church, faithful to the lessons of the Second Vatican Council, speaks of a *new evangelization of cultures*. The Gospel of Jesus Christ can mean the difference between cultures that live in hope and those that are threatened by despair.

Like people, cultures need hope to survive, for the real *humanum* yearns to construct the future. What prospects are we really facing? According to several analysts, we are presently witnessing an overall crisis in long term planning for the future. The immediate or short term dominates behavior. Have the death of ideologies and the deceptions of liberal or socialist utopias inflicted a mortal blow to the ultimate desire for a more humane society? Not often have Christians been faced with such a challenge. Who will provide the modern world with hope in view of such agonizing questions about our common future? The question is crucial, for it has to do with the frustrating sense of resignation or even fatalism experienced by so many men and women today. This is one of the most insidious temptations that traps the young and the victims of injustice, as well as all those who feel impotent when faced with the infinite complexity of social, political, economic, and international life.

This is an historic moment for Christians: the cultural anxieties of modern society challenge us to deepen the present significance of our faith and hope in Jesus Christ. This is one of the priorities of the new evangelization. For us, the values of the Gospel offer the unique solid foundation for the societies of tomorrow. Cardinal Suenens has expressed the Church's major task with this succinct formula: "The heart of the problem facing the Church today is: how can we Christianize such a vast number of nominal Christians? How can we evangelize a world which has become, to a large degree, post-Christian?"[1]

Recent experience is teaching us that the effort to implant the Gospel in cultures and social structures is a very arduous task indeed. Now we realize that implementing programs of inculturation and projects of liberation is much more complex than many of us had foreseen. One of the main reasons is that the triad—evangelization, inculturation, and liberation—cannot be arbitrarily separated. The successful evangelizer must spin the common thread out of these three elements. There is no shortcut or simplified method for proclaiming the message of Christ, for it presupposes an integrated effort of evangelization, cultural development, and the promotion of justice. Some are tempted to separate the Gospel from liberation or from inculturation, and some even separate justice from culture. This leads to the denial of the full liberating force characteristic of the Christian message. Evangelization remains unfinished if it does not achieve justice and transform cultures. It is a contradiction to view the struggle for justice in conflict with the promotion of culture, for the work of justice is one of the highest realizations of Christian humanism—really the work of civilization and the elevation of humankind. The basic needs of humankind are not only of biological or material order. They are equally spiritual and cultural. How can we defend human rights without struggling also for the cultural rights that are essential to the survival of persons and peoples? Moreover, how can we promote cultural development without guaranteeing at the same time the indispensable conditions for a social and economic life worthy of a human being?

Justice and culture call out to each other as two facets of the same desire, one that dominates our epoch. These questions have a dramatic resonance in the developing countries, but they are now also loudly debated among Christians of the so-called advanced societies. We all defend our cultural identities and our basic rights to justice and solidarity with the same vigor. Human beings certainly have essential needs to be fed, cared for, and to find shelter, with security, but they also have the vital needs to know, to comprehend the changing world, to be respected for their identity, to be able to affirm themselves and to develop within human cultures. Humankind aspires with all its might to satisfy simultaneously the fundamental needs of justice *and* culture. The Gospel is the true answer to these basic aspirations.

The final test of modernity will be precisely its openness to these transcendent values. They are the radical prerequisites that ensure for tomorrow the sheer plausibility of human culture. True liberation would be betrayed if we do not defend persons in their basic right to participate in cultural life. Promoting cultural rights has now become an urgent task for Christians and all people anxious to defend the future of human beings. Food for the human mind and soul is as vital as food for the human body.

Indeed, evangelizing modern culture is crucial, and—with the plethora of countervailing historical trends so perfectly illustrated by the plight of the peoples of the Balkans and so many ethnic conflicts erupting in all parts of the world—one might be tempted to say, "an impossible dream." Yet, the present world is the only one we have in which to bear witness to our faith in Jesus Christ, the Savior of all humankind for all time. Announcing the Gospel today is not just a pietistic effort—it is inseparable from the dual commitment to justice and cultural development. Facts show the validity of these tenets of the Christian message. The fight for justice that does not respect cultural aspiration leads to injustice. Similarly, inculturation programs that neglect the economic and political conditions of integral development are betrayals of both justice and culture. Both attitudes fall short of what the new evangelization must be about. Christian growth according to one's cultural identity is the golden rule of inculturation—for the wealthy countries as well as for those aspiring to modernization. Individuals and peoples progress only by remaining faithful to the integrity of their souls and cultures. Amnesia with regard to this fundamental human need explains the collapse in the past of many projects for development and economic recovery.

These views are widely shared today by people across religious and philosophical barriers, and it would be erroneous to think that a Catholic agenda for evangelizing cultures could contradict ecumenical or inter-religious cooperation. In the vast field of socio-economic and cultural development, Catholics have been encouraged by Vatican II to work together with other Christians, other believers, and with all people of good will for the betterment of the human condition.

Besides Christians, many people today are convinced that such evangelical values as sisterly and brotherly love, compassion for the poor, the transcendent destiny of the human person, the sacred character of the family, the solidarity of all peoples, respect for the development of nature to the benefit of all men and women, and the moral accountability of everyone before the divine Creator and Lawgiver, constitute a solid and even necessary moral basis for the construction and defense of a human society worthy of the name.

In the final analysis, it is within the secrecy of the human conscience that the Gospel transforms modes of life and the social structures of the modern world. The specific impact of the Church on cultures comes from its announcing the truth about Creation and Redemption, as John Paul II recalled in the encyclical *Centesimus Annus*:

> Thus the first and most important task is accomplished within man's heart. The way in which he is involved in building his own future depends on the understanding he has of himself and of his own destiny. It is on this level that *the Church's specific and decisive contribution to true culture* is to be found.[2]

In the present experience and teaching of the Church, the *new evangelization* is explicitly defined by its main goal: *inculturation* in its full realization. John Paul II expresses it in these words:

> The task of inculturation, as the integral diffusion of the Gospel and its subsequent translation into thought and life, still continues today and *constitutes the heart, the means and the scope of the New Evangelization.*[3]

Even if the terms *inculturation* and *new evangelization* are of recent coinage, they convey the primal conviction of Christians that the Gospel of Jesus Christ is to be announced to all generations, times, and cultures, including our own.

Facing such a mission, our proposals can only be modest. Nevertheless, they are offered as an invitation to dialogue and further research. This present book contains seven essays presented as probes into the more promising aspects of the new evangelization that announces the hope of Jesus Christ to the culture of modernity. It is directed to all persons and groups that are engaged in the difficult but indispensable mission of evangelizing modern culture for the integral liberation of all.

In editing this book I have been ably assisted by Sister Anne Clare Keeler, F.S.E., to whom I express all due gratitude.

# 1

# The Church's Perception
# of Modernity

The rapprochement between the Church and the modern world is a slow process, and it is not easy to retrace the main steps. Nevertheless, it is a certain fact that the Second Vatican Council was momentous in helping Christians acquire a new perception of modern society. We must add also that this Council has made its imprint on the culture of our time through the originality of its discernment on modernity and through the re-orientation of the Church in this regard.

Although the word *inculturation* was never used by Vatican II, what the Council has achieved in reassessing contemporary cultures can be considered an emblematic effort in inculturating the Gospel in our times.

## VATICAN II AS A CULTURAL EVENT

Viewed in a sociological perspective, Vatican II can be seen as a cultural event of historic importance, and, in a certain sense, the Council as a cultural event is as important as the statements found in its documents on culture. It can be said that after Vatican II, Catholics no longer saw the Church and the world in exactly the same way as they did before it. It is this collective cultural experience that must first be brought into focus if we are to evaluate the contribution of Vatican II to culture and to

7

the understanding of inculturation. Some original teaching on the relationship between the Church and the various cultures was of course set forth, especially in *Gaudium et Spes*, as also in other conciliar documents—and we shall stress the full significance of this—but it seems to us indispensable to understand in the first place the background and foundations of this teaching: in other words, the new attitude of mind, both theological and anthropological, that progressively grew within the Fathers of the Council as they investigated the meaning of the Church for contemporary men and women.

The cultural dimensions of the Council emerge clearly, now that a certain period of time has passed and we can examine some of its characteristics in a clearer perspective: the originality of its declared objectives, the quality and origins of the participants, and, above all, the theological-historical vision that bit by bit took on form and expression. Let us consider each of these aspects in turn, which will help us throw light on the cultural significance of Vatican II.

## ANTHROPOLOGICAL OBJECTIVES

The announcement of Vatican II by John XXIII set the anthropological tone for the forthcoming Council, when he said that its perspective would be primarily pastoral, pointing out that this would require a new and courageous effort to understand and meet with the contemporary world. John XXIII noted the dramatic distance between Church and world. The aspect of the Pope's declarations that struck the Church and the media most immediately was his benevolent attitude toward the contemporary world. He said that he was dissociating himself from those who "in these modern times . . . can see nothing but prevarication and ruin," as if the situation of the world were constantly deteriorating. "We feel we must disagree with those prophets of gloom, who are always forecasting disaster, as though the end of the world were at hand." He certainly was not ignoring any of the great problems of the Church, its internal shortcomings, its difficulties, and the persecutions it suffered. However, he was casting a gaze over the present times that was made up primarily of comprehension and appreciation, for he knew that Divine Providence is always at work in the world, mysteriously laying the groundwork for a new order of human relations: "In the present order of things, Divine Providence is leading us to a new order of human relations which, by men's own efforts and even beyond their very expectations, are directed toward the fulfilment of God's superior and inscrutable designs. And everything, even human differences, leads to the greater good of the Church."

If the Church is to be understood by this new world, we must first of all discover and provide an intelligible guise for the full and unchanging teaching of the Church: "The substance of the ancient doctrine of the deposit of faith is one thing, and the way in which it is presented is another. And it is the latter that must be taken into great consideration with patience if necessary, everything being measured in the forms and proportions of a magisterium which is predominantly pastoral in character."

The seeds of the anthropological and pastoral intuition of the whole Council are found in these words, which also indicate an approach that is more "medicinal" than disciplinary. The Church certainly in no way condones error, and when necessary knows how to condemn it clearly. However, today it prefers the medicine of mercy to that of severity, seeking to win minds through the attraction of its teaching: "Nowadays, the Spouse of Christ prefers to make use of the medicine of mercy rather than that of severity. She considers that she meets the needs of the present day by demonstrating the validity of her teaching rather than by condemnation."[1] This means calling on Christians to become visible and credible witnesses within human society.

John XXIII also issued a courageous invitation to "separated Christians" in order to ensure solid ecumenical participation in the work of the Council and involve all Christians in a shared discernment of their responsibilities toward a world that is challenging them dramatically.

The word *aggiornamento* (updating) has enjoyed great popularity and describes well the process John Paul XXIII wanted for the Council. A twofold renewal is involved. In the first place, the Church purifies and redefines itself, and, on the other hand, it makes an effort to renew its understanding of the present world. This twofold theological and anthropological approach would become the main orientation and the source of inspiration for the whole Council. However, the Fathers of the Council only gradually became aware of this. Cardinal Montini's letter to the clergy of Milan in January 1963 bears witness to the questioning attitude and the spirit of research of the Fathers:

> At the Council the Church is seeking herself, trying with great trust and a great effort to define and understand herself better as she really is. After twenty centuries of history, the Church seems to be submerged by the civilization of the world, so that she appears to be in fact absent from the contemporary world. She is therefore feeling the need for recollection, self-purification, and self-renewal, in order to be able to set out again on her own path with great energy. . . . While she is thus working to define and identify herself, the Church is also examining the world, and trying to enter into contact with contemporary society. . . . And how is this contact to take place? It means reentering into dialogue with the world, discerning the needs of the society in which it acts, observing the shortcomings, the needs, the aspirations, the sufferings, the hopes that lie within men's hearts.[2]

This urgent, anxious questioning, so clearly in the style of the future Pope Paul VI, reveals the attitude of research that inspired those who were perceptive participants in the Council.

## THEOLOGICAL-HISTORICAL APPROACH

Two attitudes were visible from the outset. On the one hand, there are the supporters of a defense of the Church *ad intra* against a hostile world that the Holy See had condemned a number of times in important documents since the nineteenth century. On the other hand, there was a group that wanted to use a new perspective in analyzing the duties of the Church toward the world, which was to be seen in its moral failings and misery, but above all in its needs and aspirations, its anguish and hope. It would be an oversimplification to say that the Council was divided into conservatives and progressives. It was more a question of different emphases in conception as to the work of the Council, as based on two different types of intellectual attitude: on the one hand, the reflection on principles, which was more accustomed to deductive methods, and, on the other, the anthropological and pastoral approach. Roger Aubert has observed: "The great confrontation of the first session of the Council was not so much between conservatives and progressives, as between notionalists and existentialists."[3]

We should bear in mind that prior to the Council, the capacity for cultural analysis was almost wholly ignored in the theological formation usually provided at the time. For the most part, the word *culture* had only an intellectual or esthetic sense, with no anthropological implications. It is indicative that the word did not appear at all in the reference tools familiar to theologians and philosophers, for example, the *Dictionnaire de Théologie Catholique* or the first editions of André Lalande's *Vocabulaire de la Philosophie* — no more than it did, for that matter, in the less recent editions of the great national encyclopedias. The majority of the Council Fathers did not yet view culture as an instrument for analyzing society, and it is hardly surprising that Vatican II should have been hesitant in accepting this point of view of anthropological analysis. It is, therefore, all the more praiseworthy that the Council came around to this idea in such a short time, thus (as we shall see in due course) updating its attitude to culture and cultures.

Some hesitation and stumbling was inevitable at the beginning of its work, so that the key theme of Vatican II, in the form of social and pastoral discernment, really only took shape toward the end of the first session, as John XXIII confided a short time before his death. It was at this point that the influence of cardinals such as Montini, Suenens, Lercaro, and König, and bishops such as Wojtyla and Garrone, was felt, and that the Council decided to turn resolutely toward the world, with its anguish, its problems of hunger and poverty, and its hopes for peace and development. By identifying itself, in the spirit of Christ, with this historical humanity, the Council came to a clear awareness of the challenge awaiting it, and thus gradually moved toward the famous Schema XIII, which would in due course, but only after some difficult debates, become one of the main texts of Vatican II: *Gaudium et Spes.*[4]

The new Pope, Paul VI, set about interpreting the effort at clarification that was then being made, when he tried to define the orientation of the Council at the opening of the second session. He assigned the Council four objectives: (1) the Church must become aware of its identity, and provide itself with "a reflected definition"; (2) the Church is called to reform itself in an awakening and in a spiritual spring; (3) the Church must reconstitute the unity of Christians in an "ecumenicity that seeks to be total and universal"; (4) the Church must reach out to today's world, "throwing a bridge across to the contemporary world." Paul VI demonstrated a very fine analytical ability, giving an excellent description of what is at stake in this dialogue with the world, as seen in all its ambivalence with regard to the Gospel. On the one hand, the Church is called to withdraw spiritually into itself, but, on the other hand, this is in order to enable it to become more effective *ad extra* as a renewing leaven for the world:

> It is a very strange phenomenon: in seeking to give fresh force to its interior life in the spirit of the Lord, it separates and sets itself apart from the profane society in which it is immersed; at the same time, however, it acts as a life-giving leaven and an instrument of salvation for this world, by discovering and reinforcing its missionary vocation, in other words, its essential task of taking humanity, whatever its condition, as the impassioned object of its evangelizing mission.[5]

These are the elements of the reflection of the new Pope, and they would then find their full expression in his Encyclical *Ecclesiam Suam*, which was promulgated during the Council (in 1964) and was devoted wholly to dialogue with the contemporary world.

## PARTICIPANTS WHO WERE OPEN TO THE PLURALITY OF CULTURES

The discovery of the world in the diversity of mentalities and cultures would be greatly stimulated by the presence of bishops from every part of the world at the Council. It was the first time that a Council included a large number of bishops from the Third World, and the point of view of the churches of Asia, Africa, and Latin America had a considerable impact on bishops from European and North American countries. Apart from this, the representatives of eastern European countries threw a stark light on the prevailing situation in the communist world.

## A NEW AWARENESS OF UNIVERSALITY

Even if the main participants at Vatican II seemed at first to be westerners and the pre-preparatory texts tended to be their work, their way of thinking certainly did not dominate the debates, so that in the course of the Council, there was a decided maturing of minds and a new awareness of universality.

This fact has been of fundamental importance in the recent life of the Church and deserves in-depth study, which should be carried out jointly by theologians and sociologists. The truly international composition of the conciliar gathering has not yet, in our opinion, been examined in a proper perspective. In a stimulating talk given in the United States, Karl Rahner attempted a first analysis, showing, with considerable nuances, how the Church truly became aware of its universal character with Vatican II. The Council was a cultural event comparable with that experienced by the first Christians when they understood, after the Council of Jerusalem, that the Gospel was to be announced to the Gentiles, which would mark the change from a "Jewish Christianity" to a "Gentile Christianity."[6]

The Council became aware of the historical internationalization of the Church, and this awareness was then called on to develop, with all the ensuing consequences. We are briefly stressing this aspect of Vatican II here, but it in fact requires a full in-depth study, similar to the one carried out by Alphonse Dupront for the Council of Trent. Dupront's socio-historical analysis of the Council of Trent sought to define the cultural significance of this conciliar event through study of the composition of its members, its aims, its reflections, and the impact it gradually had on its own period. His analysis of "the mental and spiritual fact" of Trent is very stimulating and indicates some interesting lines of research for students of Vatican II, and it is only to be hoped there will be a proliferation of similar studies on the last Council.[7]

Apart from the bishops themselves, there were other participants — the various experts, the representatives of religious and lay people, and the ecumenical observers — who made an active contribution to the particular configuration of Vatican II. Many of the experts were theologians who specialized in biblical, liturgical, and patristic renewal. There were also sociologists who were accustomed to carrying out their research within a pastoral perspective. These experts brought a rich experience of theological and historical investigation to the Council, drawn from reflection on biblical, liturgical, and pastoral renewal, the human sciences and religious sociology, and the work of Catholic Action, with its method of "seeing, judging, and acting" that had over the past twenty years awakened Catholics to an awareness of cultural analysis in the service of evangelization.

Although the interdisciplinary reflection that was a feature of collaboration between the bishops and the experts was often improvised and confusing, after a good deal of patience and perseverance, it did bear fruit, and its effects can be seen in all the major documents of the conciliar commissions. In these documents, the most traditional subjects, as well as the newer ones, are dealt with in a perspective that is both doctrinal and incarnated within time. An indication of this is found in the terminology used in the texts: the words *world, society, dialogue, service, novelty, transformation,* and *lay* appear frequently. The attention is decidedly on the present time of the world and the Church. The terms *hodie* or *hodiernus* occur 145 times. There is a constant reference to culture: the words *culture* or *cultural* appear 125 times. Lexicographical studies have noted how different the terminology of Vatican II is from that of Vatican I, in which the word *culture,* for example, occurs only once.[8]

The presence of observers from other Christian confessions represented another characteristic feature of the Council. They contributed their points of view and lent their perspectives to the whole gathering. Some of them who brought a certain amount of skepticism with them to Rome soon expressed their admiration, and also their confidence in ecumenical research and in the courageous openness of the Council to the contemporary world. Statements to this effect were made by the Secretary General of the World Council of Churches, Visser 't Hooft, and by the President of the World Methodist Council, Rev. Corson, who observed that the Council was tackling the urgent problems of the contemporary world: "I look to it to tackle particularly problems such as that of the rights and needs of the young nations, the missionary vocation of Christianity with regard to workers, religious freedom, and the responsibility of lay people."[9]

## A NEW CULTURAL AND ECCLESIAL PERCEPTION

This description of the intellectual and spiritual context enables us to understand the cultural experience lived by all those who took part in the Council. Together at the Council, they experienced a deep immersion in the affairs of the Church and the world, and they taught one another to see humanity striving to embrace the Gospel.

This collective sensitization paved the way for a deeper ecclesial awareness. Their dynamic understanding was expressed in the concept of the people of God on the move through history—an image of the pilgrim Church built up through time. This concept is both biblical and historical, and provided the ecclesiology of Vatican II with its full existential and pastoral breadth. Without in any way repudiating it, the Council went beyond the concept of the Church as a perfect society with its own special rights and clearly laid the stress on the Church within the human family as a leaven to serve humanity by evangelizing it. The history of salvation and earthly history must, therefore, be seen as a whole, inasmuch as they have the same subject—humankind in its individual and collective aspects—and also the same divine source. Faith allows us to see that "the earthly and the heavenly city penetrate each other" (*GS* 40). *Gaudium et Spes* would echo the principle of *Lumen Gentium* a number of times: "it is the same God who is at once Savior and Creator, Lord of human history and of the history of salvation" (*GS* 41).

Theologians have emphasized the central importance of the concept of the Church seen in its eschatological dynamism as this is presented in *Lumen Gentium*. With remarkable force and strong hope, the whole of Chapter VII, "The Eschatological Character of the Pilgrim Church," shows how the destiny of the Church is bound up with the liberation of the whole of humanity. We find the following statement: "the pilgrim Church, in its sacraments and institutions, which belong to this present age, carries the mark of this world which will pass, and she herself takes her place among the creatures which groan and travail yet and await the revelation of the sons of God (cf. Rom. 8:19-22)" (*LG* 48).

Even in the face of a sinful or hostile world, the Church does not set itself apart from humankind. Although it is, of course, distinct from the world, it will not allow itself to be separated from it, as Paul VI stated in *Ecclesiam Suam* and then repeated, in a formulation that conveys the full force of his conviction, at the opening of the third session on September 14, 1964: "The Church is not in itself its own end, but wants to belong wholly to Christ, through Christ, in Christ, and wholly to men, among men, and for men."[10]

We can, therefore, say that the theological perspective of Vatican II cannot be separated from its cultural perception of the contemporary world. It is not possible to conceive of the Church outside living cultures, while, on the other hand, human cultures only find true salvation in Jesus Christ. This fact led a number of informed observers of the Council to state that the major document on the Church, *Lumen Gentium*, only finds its full significance in the light of *Gaudium et Spes*, on the Church in the contemporary world. Cardinal Garrone, who presided over the maturation of *Gaudium et Spes*, recalled that it was Paul VI himself who wanted to make it a Constitution—a Pastoral Constitution, maybe, but all the same, a true Constitution, as the Pope insisted to those who had doubts about the idea. Thus, Paul VI stepped in to see that the famous Schema XIII became a Constitution equal in dignity with the other conciliar Constitutions. Cardinal Garrone observes that, in a certain sense, the whole of the Council rests on two main pillars: the first is represented by the Constitution on the Church, *Lumen Gentium*, with the other two Constitutions—on revelation and the liturgy—that complement it; and the second corresponds to the Pastoral Constitution *Gaudium et Spes*, which provides the link with the present situation of the world and which "has the precise aim of adapting *Lumen Gentium* to things as they really are . . . and to the overall problem of man within the world."[11]

No Council throughout history had placed humanity and the world at the center of its debates in this way.[12] This is the "humanism" of Vatican II, of which Paul VI would speak in unforgettable tones at the close of the Council.

## WHAT THE COUNCIL HAD TO SAY ABOUT CULTURE

The foregoing description was indispensable if we are to assess the importance of the formal teaching of Vatican II on culture. It is perhaps significant that the Constitution *Gaudium et Spes* was only approved at the end of the Council. The Fathers first needed to live through the complex experience of discernment that we have just sketched out. This suggests that their lived experience and their formal teaching should definitely not be seen as isolated from each other. Let us begin with the statements about culture found in *Gaudium et Spes* (53-62), after which we shall extend our observations to the other conciliar documents.

### A MODERN DEFINITION OF CULTURE

The remarkable thing about the definition of culture proposed by *Gaudium et Spes* is its modern character, which is borrowed from the human sciences. The two dimensions of culture are found linked in perfect harmony. On the one hand, culture is seen as concerned with the progress of the individual, who develops all his or her potential through the application of intelligence and talents. This is culture as traditionally understood in the classical and humanistic sense. A second, more modern view of culture points to the anthropological life experience and the typical mentality of each human group. This twofold dimension of culture as used in *Gaudium et Spes* allows us to understand the relationship between the culture of the individual and the cultures of groups, between scholarly culture and living cultures, for it is humanity that is the subject and the beneficiary of all cultural progress.

Let us reread the definition proposed by *Gaudium et Spes* 53, bearing in mind the whole cultural experience through which the conciliar gathering had just lived:

> The word "culture" in the general sense refers to all those things which go to the refining and developing of man's diverse mental and physical endowments. He strives to subdue the earth by his knowledge and his labor; he humanizes social life both in the family and in the whole civic community through the improvement of customs and institutions; he expresses through his works the great spiritual experiences and aspirations of men throughout the ages; he communicates and preserves them to be an inspiration for the progress of many, even of all mankind.
>
> Hence it follows that culture necessarily has historical and social overtones, and the word "culture" often carries with it sociological and ethnological connotations; in this sense one can speak about a plurality of cultures. For different scales of values originate in different ways of using things, of working and self-expression, of practicing religion and of behavior, of establishing laws and juridical institutions, of developing science and the arts and of cultivating beauty.

We are immediately struck by the fact that this text reveals a dynamic and concrete view of humanity in its historical development. The text provides a reading key for contemporary history in the form of an anthropological reflection on the progress offered to humanity, both individually and collectively. The Church thus provided itself with a modern analytical instrument in order to understand the world better and carry out its role in it. This represented a slow but decisive intellectual advance, for since Leo XIII the Church had been more accustomed to speak of "civilization," and only slowly did it come to adopt the concept of anthropological culture. Even at the time of Pius XII, culture was still understood almost exclusively in the humanistic sense.

## A CALL TO CULTURAL ANALYSIS

Let us see the sense in which the cultural approach of Vatican II brought a new eye to bear on societies. We should remember that since the great social encyclicals of Leo XIII and Pius XI and the famous Christmas addresses of Pius XII (not to mention his other writings), the Holy See had shown itself increasingly concerned with the "social question" and the problems of peace, work, capitalism, and communism. Even so, the perspective was primarily ethical, so that the labor question, the abuses of capitalist, communist, or fascist regimes, and international conflicts were judged according to moral norms or as being in opposition to "Christian civilization."[13]

Vatican I had intended dealing with a certain number of social questions, and some draft documents on such matters were indeed drawn up. However, the taking of Rome meant that the Council had to wind up its work prematurely, before it had had time to deal with these questions.[14]

All this reminds us that the Church already had a "social perception" of the modern world. However, the important point is that this social perspective still tended to take the form of moral judgment rather than sociological analysis. The originality of Vatican II would lie precisely in the fact that it took up the modern approach of anthropology, while it obviously in no way repudiated the traditional moral perspective.

The method of cultural analysis based on the human sciences made it easier to understand the collective behavior, thought patterns, dominant values, aspirations, and contradictions of our time. This anthropological approach would be seen at the Council not only as a necessary preliminary to any moral judgment on our times, but also as an indispensable prerequisite for the discovery of new cultures that are waiting for the Gospel. The Church is becoming more methodically sensitive to the signs of the times, to significant developments, and to the values and countervalues that challenge the Christian conscience.

Although a number of Catholic scholars were, of course, already using the term *culture* in its more modern sense, the official documents hardly provided the faintest echo. Then, at Vatican II, the official Church updated its view of culture almost overnight. This represented an intellectual journey similar to that made by certain international organizations such as UNESCO or the Council of Europe, which had been trying for some time to move from the traditional concept of culture to one that encompassed the anthropological dimension of living societies as well as the sphere of literature, science, and the arts.[15]

The intention of Vatican II in providing itself with a tool for cultural analysis was that of laying stress on the close link among culture, evangelization, and the mission of the Church. Let us give some references from *Gaudium et Spes* to start with, after which we can move on to a rapid survey of the other conciliar documents.

## THE CONCILIAR IMAGE OF THE WORLD AND THE CHURCH

At the beginning of *Gaudium et Spes* (Nos. 4-10), we find a cultural analysis of the contemporary world that even today seems remarkably acute. The contemporary world is described, with its hopes and fears, and also the profound changes affecting it in the social, psychological, moral, and religious spheres. This world shows points of serious imbalance, and these, in contrast, point up the universal aspirations of the human race. The Church recognizes this contemporary situation and is thus particularly attentive to the underlying questions of men and women today. It sees the world from the point of view of the Gospel and is aware of the close bonds between culture and the message of salvation: "There are many links between the message of salvation and culture. In his self-revelation to his people culminating in the fullness of manifestation in his incarnate Son, God spoke according to the culture proper to each age" (*GS* 58). The Church also understands the extent to which cultures can influence religious life, and thus cultures can themselves become the privileged locus for evangelization: "the Church has existed through the centuries in varying circumstances and has utilized the resources of different cultures in its preaching to spread and explain the message of Christ, to examine and understand it more deeply, and to express it more perfectly in the liturgy and in various aspects of the life of the faithful" (*GS* 58).

A central observation emerges quite clearly: culture is not dealt with in itself, in an abstract way; rather, the culture of contemporary humankind is always seen as the context for theological reflection and pastoral projection. This highlights one of the mainsprings of the Council: the social and theological approach that underlay all its work. We would thus be unduly minimizing its contribution to culture if we considered only the passages of *Gaudium et Spes* that deal specifically with the subject, thus seeing culture simply as one chapter among others. On the contrary, everything at the Council was concerned with culture, just as everything was concerned with theology. Contemporary and historical humanity is never absent from its concerns and reflections, and the analytical framework is always both ecclesial and cultural. This is the perspective in which we must reread and interpret the main documents of the Council on bishops, priests, religious freedom, and the media. Let us take a few representative examples.

Bishops, priests, and those responsible for the pastoral ministry are warmly called on to use the modern tools of the human sciences, and especially of psychology and sociology, in order to throw light on the cultural circumstances in which they must proclaim the Gospel (*GS* 62). Serious research in this field is strongly encouraged (*GS* 36).

Religious must seek the driving force of their original vocation and live out their charism in new cultural contexts (*PC* 3).

Lay people are to play a direct role in the affairs of the secular world, and in the fostering of cultures, so as to bear witness to their faith wherever human values are in question (*AA* 17).

In ecumenical dialogue, the cultural factors of disunion must be discovered, and from now on, all Christians must be encouraged to work together effectively in the social, economic, and cultural spheres (*UR* 12).

It is important to be able to discern the seeds of the Word hidden within the heart of non-Christian religions, and seek to integrate into an overall Christian approach all cultural values that are not in opposition to the Catholic faith (*AG* 11). It is also important that in-depth reflection should be carried out on this point in all the great socio-cultural areas (*AG* 22).

The same approach should be applied to the adaptation of

the liturgy to different cultures, while never losing sight of the norms of the universal Church in this regard. It is recommended that the gifts and characteristics of each culture should be carefully examined in order to see what can be assimilated into an authentically Christian liturgical practice (*SC* 27).

The media come in for special attention, since they have a considerable influence on culture and public morality (*IM* 12).

Faced with the formidable problem of modern atheism, the Church must reflect on the cultural conditions of belief and unbelief (*GS* 19-21).

The whole area of education is considered within a perspective of cultural development, with the aim of providing a well-rounded intellectual and spiritual formation of the young, making use of advances in psychology and teaching methods (*GE* 1).

Culture—understood as intellectual creativity—is a particularly characteristic dimension of this Council and, in a great variety of contexts, it deals with modern science, and also with its relationship to faith and human development; freedom in research; advances in teaching methods and the human sciences; the human and spiritual formation of priests, religious, and lay people; the role of schools and universities; and artistic creation. The focus is always on the person in his or her personal and collective development—a statement that could be supported by citations from almost every document.

## THE ENCOUNTER WITH THE CONTEMPORARY MENTALITY

In more general terms, we can see how attentive the Council was to the mentality of contemporary men and women, and how it sought to give full value to the typical cultural aspirations of our era, such as the desire for participation, the sense of co-responsibility, human solidarity, personal decision making, interiorization, and religious freedom, as well as the responsibility of lay people, the role of women, the importance of the young, and the universal search for justice, peace, and development for all human beings. These social and pastoral interests can be seen in all the documents as a very practical concern in relation to evangelization. Let us take a look at some of the passages that are concerned especially with pastoral life.

Modern men and women are very conscious of their freedom and personal rights, and in addressing them, the Council emphasizes the free choice of the believer. The rule that religious adherence corresponds to a free commitment on the part of the individual is constantly recalled. This is one of the fundamental principles of the Declaration of Religious Freedom: "the practice of religion of its very nature consists primarily of those voluntary and free internal acts by which a man directs himself to God. Acts of this kind cannot be commanded or forbidden by any merely human authority" (*DH* 3). This also applies to the Christian's act of faith: "The act of faith is of its very nature a free act. . . . The principle of religious liberty contributes in no small way to the development of a situation in which men can without hindrance be invited to the Christian faith, [and] embrace it of their own free will" (*DH* 10).

The critical spirit so typical of modern culture can undoubtedly represent a threat to a superficial faith, but equally it can purify the religious spirit: "a more critical ability to distinguish religion from a magical view of the world and from the superstitions which still circulate purifies religion and exacts day by day a more personal and explicit adherence to faith. As a result many persons are achieving a more vivid sense of God" (*GS* 7).

Participation in the liturgy must be conscious and personal: "Mother Church earnestly desires that all the faithful should be led to that full, conscious, and active participation in liturgical celebrations which is demanded by the very nature of the liturgy," and liturgical reform must aim at this type of active and personal participation as a primary objective (*SC* 14).

The human sciences should be used so that pastoral action can be better adapted not only to the spiritual conditions, but also to the social, demographic, and economic circumstances of different peoples. A great contribution can be provided by "social and religious research conducted by institutes of pastoral sociology, the establishment of which is strongly recommended" (*CD* 16-17).

Lay people are encouraged to express their opinion freely within the Church and to play an active role in research, so that

they can serve it better: "By reason of the knowledge, competence and pre-eminence which they have, the laity are empow-
ered—indeed sometimes obliged—to manifest their opinions on
those things which pertain to the good of the Church" (*LG* 37).

In more general terms, Catholics must make an effort to
understand their historical period: "the faithful ought to live in
close conjunction with their contemporaries and try to get to
know their ways of thinking and feeling, as they find them
expressed in current culture" (*GS* 62). This is a necessary prerequisite for dialogue between the Gospel and culture, which
requires careful research:

> Let the faithful incorporate the findings of new sciences
> and teachings and the understanding of the most recent
> discoveries with Christian morality and thought, so that
> their practice of religion and their moral behaviour may
> keep abreast of their acquaintance with science and the
> relentless progress of technology: in this way they will suc-
> ceed in evaluating and interpreting everything with an
> authentically Christian sense of values (*GS* 62).

We believe that this rapid overview shows one of the most
original elements of this Council—its cultural, historical, and
anthropological focus. In his closing speech, Paul VI made a
point of stating with remarkable emphasis that this Council had
been devoted, above all, to humanity: "All this doctrinal wealth
has but one aim: that of serving man, and here we obviously
mean all men, whatever their condition, their sufferings and
their needs." When emphasizing "the human value of the Council," he appealed to the modern spirit for understanding, since
our period judges everything on the basis of its utility to humanity. This cultural view of humanity is no way abstract or theoretical, but pastoral: "Our humanism becomes Christianity."
Through "the face of every man—especially when tears and
sufferings have made it more transparent—we can and must
recognize the face of Christ." The whole Council is summed up
in this religious conclusion, he adds: "It is nothing other than a
friendly and pressing appeal, urging humanity to rediscover God
through the path of brotherly love."[16]

## EVALUATION AND FUTURE PROSPECTS

With a view to providing a further projection of our analysis, we shall make three observations that will help to situate the contribution of the Council within a socio-historical perspective.

1. The outstanding event that took place in the Second Vatican Council was that of making the whole Church aware of a modern approach to cultural changes as these are experienced by contemporary men and women. The Council Fathers became acquainted with the different cultures, with their amazing potential, their contradictions and conflicts, and above all their deep-seated aspirations for peace, justice, and brotherhood. This sensitization on both an intellectual and spiritual level is a gain from which the whole Church has benefited and which it can never again go back on. It is an indispensable form of evangelical discernment enabling us to understand the evolving societies of today in their unceasing shared quest for justice and dignity. This attitude of mind and this attention to different cultures represent a fundamental step forward taken by Vatican II. It constitutes a true advance in the capacity for discernment, which is undoubtedly far more important than the concrete description and historical reflections the Council has left us, as concerns present cultures. Indeed, the social analysis of the Council Fathers can still be improved on, and now, thirty years later, we can recognize its inevitable shortcomings as we are struck by new cultural problems calling for the attention of the Church today.

2. Since the mid-1960s, many cultural questions have arisen about which it would obviously have been impossible for Vatican II to have said much. The subsequent teaching of Paul VI and John Paul II, and the reflections of the various synods and ecclesial communities, would give these problems an important place on their agendas.

As an example, we would mention the very contemporary question of inculturation, which is at the center of lively debates in the churches of Africa, Asia, and Latin America, but also in the older churches. Vatican II was not unaware of the problems underlying the question of inculturation, although it only considered the question in general terms (cf. *GS* 58). Indeed, the term *inculturation* was never even used by the Council, although it had been in current use among Catholics for at least thirty years.[17] It was not until the 1977 synod that the word made its appearance in an official text of the Church.[18]

We should also remember the whole debate aroused by the evangelization of cultures, which the 1974 synod would in due course describe as one of the priorities of the Church. Paul VI's Apostolic Exhortation *Evangelii Nuntiandi*, which followed this synod in 1975 — ten years after Vatican II — would provide what has been called a true charter for the evangelization of cultures. In this document, Paul VI was, of course, drawing inspiration from Vatican II, but he greatly clarified its analysis, translating it into more practical lines of action.

Another contemporary concern is the question of cultural policies pursued by modern governments in the name of humanism that may be very praiseworthy in many cases, but that in others is in danger of becoming a form of ideological manipulation. There is a challenge here for Christians that was only considered indirectly by the Council (*GS* 59).

Let us also mention the various questions linked to cultural development, cultural liberation, and cultural rights, all of which are major issues in social policies and action.

The Council was not able to foresee and deal with everything. However, if we reread its teachings in the perspective of present-day problems, we can find principles that can provide us with useful guidelines in the search for solutions. In the first place, we can recognize an analytical approach that makes it possible to set about dealing with new problems with a modern sense of realism and in a spirit of objective research, which is a necessary precondition for any sure discernment.

3. While recognizing the original contribution of Vatican II to culture, we must in all honesty place its contribution within the context of a long historical tradition. We should remember, for instance, the work of Leo XIII, who was so concerned over the changes in Christian civilization in his time, and also that of Pius XI — the pontiff whose Encyclical *Divini Illius Magistri* on education (1929) brought about the reform of Catholic universities and faculties. We should also think of Pius XII, whose

exceptional mind did not ignore any of the more important human questions of his day. Even so, as we have already noted, until Vatican II, the official Church was more interested in speaking of *civilization* than of *culture*, and it was only at the Council that the language of anthropologists and cultural sociologists was adopted.

Within this historical perspective, we must also note that the movement has continued apace since Vatican II. Research on new cultural problems has undeniably become both broader and deeper with the passing of time.

The most noteworthy and promising recent development is the ability shown by the Church to translate the intuitions and declarations of the Council into terms of practical action. Paul VI and John Paul II have played an energetic role in this progress. For the sake of brevity, we shall confine ourselves to two particularly important points. Paul VI and John Paul II have in a sense dramatized what is at stake in the dialogue of the Church with present-day cultures, and have tried to make the involvement of Catholics in the service of cultures an active one.

For his part, Paul VI wanted the Synod on Evangelization in 1974 to study the difficult but pressing question of the *evangelization of cultures*, which he saw as the major drama of our age. Let us recall his words, which were so full of both concern and hope: "The split between the Gospel and culture is without a doubt the drama of our time, just as it has been in other times. Therefore every effort must be made to ensure a full evangelization of culture, or more correctly of cultures."[19]

It will be recalled that John Paul II took another step forward when, at the beginning of his pontificate, he proposed the creation of a department of the Holy See in Rome that was to deal with relations between the Church and the various cultures. After study and reflection, he therefore decided in 1982 to establish the Pontifical Council for Culture, with the precise task of implementing the orientations of Vatican II and translating *Gaudium et Spes* into a practical program for the whole Church. He was also aware of how much was at stake here. In the letter establishing the Pontifical Council for Culture, he stated: "Since the beginning of my pontificate, I have considered the Church's dialogue with the cultures of our time to be a vital area, one in which the destiny of the world at the end of this twentieth century is at stake." He went on to say that the mission of the new council would be that of implementing the cultural objectives of Vatican II: "For this reason, it seems to me opportune to found a special permanent body for the purpose of promoting the great objectives which the Second Vatican Ecumenical Council proposed regarding the relations between Church and culture."[20]

If we look at the tasks that John Paul II has assigned to this Council for Culture — and in a wider sense to the whole Church — we can gain an idea of the extent of the mission awaiting Catholics within the newly emerging cultures. All the various institutions and sectors of the Church are urged to cooperate in this mission: the Roman curia, dioceses, Catholic organizations, religious, universities, and centers for research and cultural animation. Christians must give their attention to all the contemporary problems of culture: the progress of the intellectual disciplines and the arts, as well as the cultural policies of governments, the cultural conditions of the development of different peoples, and the activity of international organizations such as UNESCO, the Council of Europe, and the various bodies dealing with science, culture, and education. The whole Church must learn to recognize the new horizons of evangelization as represented by living cultures. It may be pointed out that this is an enormous task, but everything is basically encompassed in the fruitful approach inspired by Vatican II.

# 2

# Modernity as a Culture to Evangelize

There were decisive moments in history when Christians felt immersed in the agony of a civilization in crisis, yet they had the strong feeling that their faith could give inspiration and shape to the culture to come.

It is a similar challenge that confronts us today as we experience the crisis of modernity. Vatican II has dedicated one of its major documents, *Gaudium et Spes,* to this question, but we have to recognize that the message of the Council on the Church and today's culture has still to be effectively implemented. A hopeful sign is the growing sensitivity in the Church concerning the dialogue between faith and cultures. In fact, a new cultural and spiritual awareness is developing among Catholics, as they try to face the extremely difficult but fascinating task of bringing the values of the Gospel to modern cultures as they are evolving toward unknown forms. The main objective consists, first, in analyzing thoroughly and understanding the cultural traits of the modern world and, second, in discovering concretely how Christian values can purify, inspire, and enrich emerging cultures. The real problem is to grasp, from a Christian point of view, what modernity is all about, inasmuch as it represents the typical culture of our epoch.

Since Vatican II, we have come to realize that a fresh dialogue with the world of today is decisive for the future of the Church. This is the reason John Paul II, who had been directly involved in these discussions during the Council, declared:

"Since the beginning of my pontificate I have considered the Church's dialogue with the cultures of our time to be a vital area, one in which the destiny of the world at the end of this twentieth century is at stake."[1]

The central problem can be stated in these terms: How can modern cultures discover Jesus Christ and his message of liberation for the men and women of our times? John Paul II urges all Christians to dedicate themselves with intelligence and generosity to that research.

> You must help the Church to respond to these fundamental questions for the cultures of today: How is the message of the Church accessible to the new cultures, to contemporary forms of understanding and of sensitivity? How can the Church of Christ make itself understood by the modern spirit, so proud of its achievements and at the same time so uneasy for the future of the human family? Who is Jesus Christ for the men and women of today?[2]

How can we believers make ourselves understood by the modern spirit? Motivated by our faith in Jesus Christ, we urgently need to investigate what constitutes precisely the culture of modernity. In the present chapter, we shall attempt an analysis of modernity from the *psycho-social point of view,* considering the repercussions of modernization on the collective conscience of our contemporaries, in an effort to discern the spiritual needs of advanced societies, as they are called.

From the outset, *modernity* is seen here as a state of mind, a mentality or a *culture* that challenges the Church, an approach that was in fact proposed by *Gaudium et Spes.*[3] We must admit that the concepts are difficult to pin down and that they carry an ideological overload that can easily lead us astray in our analysis. The terms most frequently used in this connection, *modernity* and *progress,* are indispensable, but they cannot be strictly defined. Insofar as modernity is opposed to tradition, a dichotomy between "modern" and "retrograde" is subtly set up in people's minds, and modernity thus comes to have a normative and idealized sense, since it is obvious that nobody wants to be considered retrograde. Reality then becomes confused with myth: modernity is a new and totalizing mentality that involves every aspect of life, personal and social, material and spiritual. These difficulties invite us to approach the phenomenon of modernity through careful cultural analysis.[4]

## MODERNITY UNDERSTOOD THROUGH THE PROCESS OF MODERNIZATION

If we are to grasp the culture of modernity, it is useful and illuminating to start with the very *fact of modernization,* which has socially observable criteria. This process can be historically identified through its traits and its effects on human societies. We shall try to sum up the description of modernization offered by sociologists, devoting particular consideration to the ways in which the progress of science and the technical changes of the industrial revolution, followed by the urban revolution, have affected the spirit of the populations that have been not only their witnesses, protagonists, and beneficiaries, but often also their victims.

### Modernization Related to Christianity

We must make a brief preliminary observation which should be kept in mind throughout this analysis: modernization is a historical experience that can be explained only in the perspective of its relationship to a Christian cultural milieu. Modernization is a phenomenon that originated in Europe, and the Christian culture of that continent has provided both a positive and a negative frame of reference. On the one hand, modern science had its origins in the Church. We should not forget that Galileo, Newton, and Descartes spoke as much of God as of the physical universe. Science successively separated itself from the Church and, in the Age of the Enlightenment, rationalist science set itself up in opposition to theology and the Christian tradition. Even in the nineteenth century, science was often confused with an anti-Christian scientism. These observations remind us of the fundamental fact that modernization has unfolded in the context of an ambivalent tension with the Church. This tension has increased in different ways, according to varying historical and geographical circumstances, and it still constitutes a challenge to Christians, who are not resigned to becoming estranged from the modern world. Today the scientific world, and also the Church itself, are in the process of reconsidering more serenely the tense relations of the past, recognizing honestly the errors and misunderstandings of both parties. The revision of the Galileo Affair, wanted by John Paul II, is a typical illustration of this new attitude.[5]

These remarks will suffice to underline the fact that modernity is indeed related to Christianity and remains a challenge for the Catholics of today. We are then invited to examine the features of the modern spirit in order to reach the hearts and minds of our contemporaries. An ethics and theology for modern times have yet to be produced. The observations that follow have the sole aim of raising significant questions for Christian reflection and action.

Let us start from a sociological description of modernization and see how it took place with the scientific, industrial, and urban revolution in eighteenth-century England and then in nineteenth-century France. This socio-historical overview is meant to introduce us to the cultural analysis of modernity. The advent of modernization can be understood on the basis of four main observations generally retained by sociologists.

## THE IMPACT OF SCIENCE AND TECHNOLOGY

In the first place, it was progress in the sciences and technology that made the industrial revolution possible. But the decisive development depends on the move from scientific discoveries to their technical utilization. The sciences transform work and productivity when they become empirical and useful. For example, electrical magnetism and thermodynamics had been known since ancient times, but it was the invention of electric motors and steam engines that marked the beginning of industrialization. To start with, it was simply a question of applying the driving force of steam or electricity to an automatic and repetitive mechanism. Although this invention is simple to our modern eyes, it revolutionized age-old habits of human work. The prodigious development of the sciences of physics, chemistry, and biology then led to a rise in the industrial and agricultural spheres that transformed all economic activity and every aspect of life. Technical and cultural changes go hand in hand, as we shall underline.

The objective of the industrialized world became rationalized and maximized production, so that the economic value of work came to be given precedence over the human value of the worker, leading to a psycho-social revolution that our contemporaries have not yet brought satisfactorily under control.

Moreover, scientific progress signaled an increasingly sharp break with traditional knowledge concerning nature and the human being. Physics rejected the biblical cosmogonies, and the human sciences provided a new, empirical, and positivist image of the human being. Comte, Freud, and Marx have had a lasting influence on the view of modern people, both individually and collectively. The impact of this scientific revolution on cultures still requires more accurate consideration.

## MOBILITY OF PERSONS AND CAPITAL

In the stable societies of the past, people and fortunes used to move slowly, since economic life was to a large extent bound up with the earth. However, everything changed with industrialization. Mobility of persons and capital was one consequence of the manufacturing concentration that soon accompanied a commercial and financial centralization. Fortunes became liquid, and capital was soon in movement, to be invested in nascent industries.

Population had previously for the most part been rural, but now people flocked toward manufacturing centers, drawn by the lure of earnings. Men, women, and children began to sell their labor, but without any clearly defined contractual protection. In a headlong and uncontrolled movement toward urbanization, the first working-class living areas appeared. These were conglomerations of human congestion and overcrowding, more than orderly communities, and their appalling material and moral destitution, described by P. Gaskell in England (1833) and L. R. Villermé in France (1840), provided the breeding ground for the first labor conflicts and the revolutionary agitation of Marx and Engels. In historical terms, modern urbanization was a destabilizing element for traditional communities, particularly the family. Besides this, immigrants in industrial towns lost their vital link with nature, its rhythms and its regulating symbolism, which are organizing elements of every religiously based traditional culture. The repercussions of this loss have not yet received sufficient analysis.

On the other hand, it must be admitted that the city represents a cultural conquest and makes a positive contribution to civilization. Lewis Mumford is correct when he states: "The city as one finds it in history is the point of maximum concentration for the power and culture of a community. . . . With language itself, it remains man's greatest work of art."[6] However, it is still true that even in the most highly urbanized countries, urban life involves glaring contradictions, and we are still a long way from the "intentional urbanization" that would make modern cities into humanly fulfilling communities.

## EMERGENCE OF THE MODERN STATE

Another aspect of modernization has been the emergence of the centralized, bureaucratic, representative State. The State came to perform a function necessary for regulating the economic and social activities of groups with divergent interests, but it tended to become an abstract power, increasingly distinct from society, a phenomenon that Marx and Engels spoke out against as a fundamental defect of modern government, which places itself artificially above real society, "creating the illusion that the affairs of the State belong to the people."[7] However we may judge these criticisms, it is undeniable that our contemporaries still have to face a serious crisis in civil authority; they have a confused attitude in view of the exorbitant claims of the State as providence, which tends to become master not only of the law but also of the economy, education, culture, communications, health, and demography, not to mention the ups and downs of ideologized politics that plague modern totalitarian countries. In every country, the State has extended its power in growing tension with real society. A serious gulf has been created between the political class and living collectivities.

## INDIVIDUALIZATION OF PERSONS

The rise of individualization is another accompanying phenomenon of modernization. The increased mobility of people and the promiscuity of urban collectivities cut individuals off from the communities to which they traditionally belonged: the village, the parish, the family. The desire for autonomy exalted individuals, who henceforth tried freely to choose their roles in society, whereas previously these roles were assigned by their milieu, age, family, and social condition.

The individual acquired a new status and freedom within society. This phenomenon was brought about not only by the effects of the industrial and urban revolution that progressively took over in Europe, but also by the currents of thought springing from romanticism, the Enlightenment, and the various philosophies that preached the ideal of a deeper awareness of freedom and a vigorous proclamation of individual rights. These claims were primarily concerned with the liberation of the individual and called the person to greater creativity and autonomy. These tendencies were notably reinforced by the spirit of Protestantism, with deep consequences on social, economic, and political attitudes, as Max Weber has explained. For all these reasons, the person became more self-conscious and tended toward greater self-affirmation. The modern mentality has taken over the positive value of these aspirations to freedom and self-fulfillment, and this represented a cultural advancement which led to the promotion of the person's rights and dignity. Moreover, the advent of the democratic spirit, together with the desire for autonomy, mobility, and the enrichment of individuals, acted as a powerful impulse toward generalized education, which is another key factor in social, cultural, economic, and political development. But individualization can also degenerate into narrow individualism. Our historical experience has shown us the tragedy of persons and societies when selfish individualism becomes dominant, leading to sheer subjectivism and the undermining of human communities.

A particularly striking consequence of individualization is the crisis in traditional institutions and communities. The transformation of the institution of the family is emblematic. The family is now increasingly conditioned by the autonomy of the individual at work and in society. The family is losing its traditional educational role and its productive and economic functions. It is breaking away from the extended family and becoming mobile, like the labor market. It is limiting births, thus striking demography a blow that may prove fatal for many western ethnic groups. The family is becoming a "haven of privacy," serving as a shelter for the individual in the midst of an impersonal society.

The crisis of the family is one of the most typical features of modernization, and it has been growing worse over the past hundred years, so that we have reached a point today where the very future of the institution of the family is being put into question through the rejection of civilly or religiously sanctioned marriage, by the phenomenon of juvenile cohabitation, the rise in the divorce rate, and growing practices of sterilization and abortion, and the spread of homosexuality as a way of life and a new subculture.

If we take the foregoing brief sociological observations as our basis, we are already in a position to attempt a description of the main cultural implications and consequences of modernization as they appeared from the outset, with effects that in a sense have continued down to our times and that will soon appear in the developing nations.

## THE CULTURAL CONSEQUENCES OF MODERNIZATION

When considering the cultural consequences of industrial modernization, we shall pay particular attention to the following phenomena: (a) a disorganized concentration of workers and their families in urbanized areas; (b) a change in relations between town and country; (c) the separation between workplace and place of residence; (d) an ever-increasing division of work according to trades, tasks, and actual types of industry; (e) the growth of a class-consciousness in which workers are placed in opposition to those owning capital; (f) the subjection of workers to an increasingly rationalized production system, which would later be aggravated by Taylorism and would give rise to a feeling of alienating, meaningless dependence, inasmuch as the worker is compelled to carry out the compartmentalized operations of what Georges Friedmann calls "work reduced to crumbs" (*le travail en miettes*); (g) the setting up of bureaucratic and anonymous relations between individuals, groups, and the centralized State.

The industrial revolution was therefore just as much a cultural revolution, and it profoundly shook a system of values that had been secure until then—values such as the significance of personal and community work, the direct relationship between humans and nature, being a member of a family that acted as support both in cohabitation and in work, the place of the individual in local and religious communities with human dimensions, and the participation in the traditions, rites, ceremonies, and celebrations that provided the major moments in life with meaning. Industrialization led to a disorganized, congested overcrowding of populations, thus striking these age-old values a serious blow, without replacing them with human communities capable of integrating and assimilating new cultures.

Never before had the human family experienced such a cultural upheaval and such a traumatic anxiety facing the unknown, which Alvin Toffler aptly described as future shock. Many times in history uncontrolled change had threatened traditional communities, but never had the crisis been so deep and far-reaching in its cultural and spiritual consequences.

The breadth of these changes has set before the Church hitherto unknown problems in its relations with society and its methods of evangelization. This historical evolution has created the modern world, with all its positive advantages, but at a very high price in human and spiritual terms. What will be the impact of modernization in the developing countries?

Today when people are trying to modernize Third World countries, they have a better understanding of the advantages of industrialization as well as its risks and its costs in human terms. The experience of the last two centuries has shown that modernization requires certain technical, social, and political conditions. Today we must, from the very start, bear in mind the relations between social and economic partners both at home and abroad, and among these partners there are now highly industrialized countries and others that are only in the very first stages of industrialization. Apart from this, it is nec-

essary to conform with existing national legislation and international agreements, such as those of the International Labor
Office. These elements come from two centuries of human experience and cannot be ignored. In the light of several decades of
development, it can be foreseen that industrialization in the
emerging countries will lead to deep cultural changes affecting
individuals, families, local communities, and traditions, and that
these changes will be no less far-reaching than those that have
been affecting western societies since the nineteenth century. It
is to be hoped that the cultural dimensions of industrialization
will receive at least as much attention as is devoted to specifically
economic objectives—an indispensable condition, if modernization of the developing countries is to be a true factor of human
as well as economic progress for the community of nations as
well as for individuals.[8] The importance of what is at stake here
invites us to carry out a critical examination of the culture of
modernity as it appears in its positive and negative effects within
the historical process of modernization.

## THE CULTURE OF MODERNITY ASSESSED

It cannot be denied that modern culture has provided humanity with advantages that no previous period had even dared hope
for. Our age feels a very special pride and legitimate satisfaction
over the leap in quality and the incredible number of scientific
and technical discoveries brought about by modern research.
Thirty years ago, Price noted that, contrary to our epoch, everything yesterday seemed stationary, and he observes that
"eighty to ninety percent of all the scientists who have ever
existed are alive today."[9] Our contemporaries are literally fas-
cinated by the advances in technology, electronics, and discoveries that have vastly improved the living conditions of so-called
affluent societies—advances covering the spheres of nutrition,
health, education, communications, transport, and above all, the
explosion in the distribution of consumer goods of every type.

However, along with this feeling of pride and admiration for
technical progress, modernity inspires as much fear as fascination. Deep-rooted misgivings are arising in the minds of our
contemporaries. Modern culture may be wonderful in its crea-

tions, but in its wake it brings contradictions and latent threats that rack the uneasy collective unconscious.

## THE MYTH OF PROGRESS AND DISILLUSIONMENT

This generalized anxiety can, to a large extent, be explained by the breakdown of the myth of irreversible progress. For a long time, a certain ideal of progress provided the inspiration for the development of industrial societies. We are now seeing the collapse of an ideology that represented the uncritical hope of the peoples of the western world for almost two centuries. We are witnessing the death of the utopia of progress, which was based on a common belief in the secure advent of a happy society, thanks to the establishment of empirical rationality and the final victory of reason and justice. One of the leaders of modern British sociology, Morris Ginsberg, has given a good description of the origin and evolution of this ideology. Eighteenth-century thinkers, he observes, viewed progress as a movement toward reason and justice while placing equality at the very center of justice.[10] Certainly a society founded on virtue and religion had been the ideal of all reformers from the time of the prophets of Israel, including Aristotle and even the proponents of the American Revolution ("In God we trust"). However, the predominant political thinking of the nineteenth century rejected the postulates of morals and religion, replacing them with a rationalist ethics, self-confidently sure of its mastery of the future.

### Rationalization Revisited

It was hoped and envisaged that when rationalization was applied to industrial production and public administration, it would lead to a society of general well-being, in which fulfillment of the individual would go hand in hand with the prosperity of nations. Later on, a number of theoreticians of development would have no hesitation over systematizing the stages in the progress of nations, in a style that was an ambiguous mixture of empirical description and idealized forecast. In 1960, for example, W. Rostow was still confidently describing the five phases in development as follows: the change in societies from their *traditional* state to the *preliminary* condition of development (instruction, spirit of enterprise, capitalization), then *take-off*, the progress to *maturity,* and lastly, *mass consumption.*[11] This is an evolutionary and overly restricted view of development, seen as the simple application of the "strategic factors" of progress, without taking sufficient account of collective psychologies, internal cultural factors, and international influences.

The myth of progress eventually turned out to be deceptive, but for more than a century it drew the so-called liberal societies as well as nations with socialist systems under its spell, although the latter were slower to recognize the cooling down of progressist ideology. In 1981 Leonid Brezhnev professed his unshakable confidence as follows: "Socialism is constantly moving forward. This is not simply a belief: we are certain of it. We shall reach our supreme objective of building a communist society. We are convinced of this because we believe in the sacred truth of our ideals."[12] Whether this type of proclamation comes from the left or the right, it cuts very little ice today, especially with the young.

### A Fresh Look at Progress

Under the pressure of events, if not through some rational reevaluation, the criticism of progress has gradually taken root in people's minds and is now recognized as a primary objective by the human sciences and philosophy. Common wisdom has also grown more critical. Beside the very valid hopes raised by modernization, which go by the names of development, liberation, and human promotion, ordinary people are increasingly disillusioned by the disappointments of progress and false rationality. With a sense of anguish, our generation is experiencing the human feeling of limitation, precariousness, and transitoriness. History no longer automatically works in our favor, and past and future catastrophes, says Adorno, have opened our eyes: "After the catastrophes of the past and in view of those to come, it would be cynical to claim that a universal plan ordered towards the good can be discerned in history, providing it with its coherence."[13]

The dominant values of modernity are seen more clearly today in all their ambivalence, giving rise to feelings of both attraction and repulsion, fascination and disillusionment. Recent history and lived experience, especially since the last war, have confused our image of the human being. Well-known thinkers had indeed been speaking out against the pitfalls of modernity from the beginning of the century: Spengler, Ortega y Gasset, Huizinga, Horkheimer, Heidegger, Husserl, Maritain, and Guardini. But we needed the harsh lesson of events before their warnings made any impression on people's awareness. Until recently, modern society had viewed individuals, rationality, pluralism, social communications, mass consumption, technology and science as indisputable values and, on the psychosocial level, they are still the driving forces for hoped for progress. However, serious countervalues have arisen, highlighting their limitations and contradictions dramatically. We shall confine ourselves to noting a few facts that underline this descending dialectic and give rise to serious moral and spiritual questioning.

## RATIONALITY VERSUS REASON

It is, for example, admitted that rationality has transformed traditional societies by providing them with productive, administrative, commercial, and financial means that are infinitely more efficient than those of the past, and nobody would want to give up this progress in order to move back into the past. However, rationality has introduced the technical and bureaucratic system that has depersonalized work and most of the relations between persons in social, economic, and political life. It is worth examining the mechanism of this psychological change.

The rationalization of production and management has revolutionized the psychology of the worker. It has led to the division of operations into sequential, repetitive, sectorial, and interdependent processes, which in turn requires that workers on whatever level play an abstract, impersonal, and interchangeable role. This cultural evolution in the workplace has made mass production and consumption possible, but it leaves those working within the system increasingly dissatisfied. Young people in particular no longer want to enter unquestioningly into this productive and administrative world, and refuse to work in places that restrict their possibilities of personal development. This is one of the added causes swelling the ranks of the young unemployed.

By giving pride of place to efficiency and maximized productivity, the technical society has fostered a schizophrenic tendency in behavior. Individuals are forced to play segmented and frustrating roles. As producers, they perform work that is reduced to tasks cut off from the final overall product. As voters, they feel increasingly incapable of grasping the complexity of public affairs. Rationality has supplanted reason, the understanding of overall objectives, and the value of personalized reflection. "Leave your personal life aside" seems to be the message of modern business, government offices, supermarkets, unions, and political parties. Everybody must be treated in the same anonymous way and with the same "objectivity" by modern administrative offices, and the experts in the system add that this has to be so for reasons of efficiency and impartiality.

By a strange paradox, the affluent society has brought about a new form of alienation in which anonymous individuals are treated artificially as simple consumers, producers, electors, and taxpayers. The contradiction becomes intolerable when the economic system is streamlined to the point that it brings about what is referred to as technological unemployment, leaving millions of people unemployed and socially emarginated. This contradiction represents an explosive situation. The economy cannot hope to keep making "progress" for long while sacrificing the "human factor." The social and economic reorganization that is indispensable seems to run counter to the rationale now in force in the economic planning of most countries.

## INDIVIDUALISM AND THE LONELY CROWD

Individualization appears to be both a value and a qualified victory. It is indeed the free individual who has provided the conditions for democracy, the spirit of enterprise, freedom of expression, the demand for equal justice for all, the need for education, and a generalized sharing in the benefits of culture. These aspirations carry modern society forward, and the young nations strive toward them with all their might, despite a great many obstacles and dramatic setbacks. On the path to overall development, Christians cannot but rejoice at the encouragement of free and responsible individuals within society. Vatican II recognized the decidedly positive aspects of a culture that encouraged personalization, greater participation, and the free involvement of individuals in the social, political, and religious spheres.[14] But *excessive* insistence on the self-interest and autonomy of the individual becomes destructive for communities and persons.

### Individualism as a Dominant Value

The negative aspects of radical individualization are glaring. The cult of the individual has destroyed the sense of tradition, undermined the institution of the family, and left individuals defenseless within a leveling pluralism. For thousands of years, people have lived in conformity with respected customs and traditions, finding a popular wisdom and supporting culture in them.[15] Today no tradition is safe from attack. Sociologist Alvin Gouldner has provided a good description of this characteristic tendency of the "new intellectuals," which is now widespread throughout society, referring to it as the "culture of critical discourse" (CCD). It constitutes a mental structure that, on principle, rejects any argument from authority or any received truth: there is no institution, tradition, or person that can state or transmit anything to us that cannot be placed in question; everything is hypothetical, and the opinion and acceptance of the recipient alone are to be recognized. "It is not only a subversion of the present, but a revolution in permanence that is grounded in the culture of critical discourse."[16] It is no longer simply an attitude for free criticism, or even of free thought, but the total emancipation of the individual with regard to every system, doctrine, or creed.

It is in this cultural context that a-religious people are now asserting themselves, under the illusion that they are freeing themselves by casting down the last of the gods, as Mircea Eliade has acutely observed: "Man *makes himself,* and he can make himself completely only to the extent that he desacralizes himself and the world. The sacred is the supreme obstacle in the path of freedom. He will only become himself at the moment when he is radically demystified. He will only be truly free at the moment when he has killed the last god."[17]

### What Type of Pluralism?

People then enter the lonely crowd made up of a multitude of anonymous individuals retreating into themselves, with their own preferred interests and values, learning with difficulty to live in a cultural milieu characterized by a plurality of absolutes, where each person affirms his or her own reasons for living. We should note that the cultural pluralism of modern society has decidedly positive aspects, if it fosters freedom of belief, comprehension of others, acceptance of minorities, tolerance, and the wish to advance a social order that respects the differences and diversities inseparable from modern society.

These advantages being recognized, an overly passive acceptance of pluralism entails the risk of destroying people's free choice, while a new mass conformism, an unconsidered consumption of goods and ideas, and cultural leveling to the lowest common denominator tend to prevail. Herbert Marcuse has observed this paradoxical phenomenon that leads to a new cultural hegemony that dominates the "one-dimensional man." A sort of harmonious pluralism imposes itself on the public. The most contradictory values and truths coexist in peace and general indifference.

These attitudes are disseminated by a large fraction of the "new intellectuals" who earn their living in the production of knowledge and information. This "new class," as it is often called, constitutes a rising power and is tending to predominate in research, the media, and the educational system. It exhibits a much more pronounced secularization and agnosticism than is found in the population as a whole, leading to a growth in conflicts and tensions between the producers of culture and its consumers. This sullen rebellion is the reason for the intensification of the school crisis in many countries. Citizens are trying to defend themselves against the slow degeneration to which the living culture that is their heritage is being subjected. This form of cultural reductionism is considerably aggravated by the persuasive pressure of modern communication, another truly revolutionary creation of our era.

## COMMUNICATIONS THAT UNITE AND DISINTEGRATE

Social communications should be understood first as a value and a cultural product and, in this perspective, the modern media have projected us into another dimension of time and space. Instantaneous communication by radio, telephone, television, cable, and satellite has created a universalized human network and an interdependence such as the inhabitants of the earth could never have dreamt, except in pure fantasy. The amazement is still with us, and we are now pondering the consequences of these extraordinary capacities to communicate with one another. From the start, it led to a stimulating feeling of universal solidarity and potential co-responsibility for the affairs of the whole planet.

### Cultural Frontiers Disappear

The traditional frontiers that had for centuries been so important in protecting national cultures have given way in the face of the irresistible encroachment of the airwaves that carry the messages, images, advertisements, and appeals of radio and television into free space. We tell ourselves that this invasion of our frontiers and our own homes is the price we pay for modernity, and we marvel that all men and women are potentially linked to their brothers and sisters. Everybody is offered the same information, works of art, knowledge, and unlimited opportunities to share in the universal cultural heritage. Data banks and personalized terminals are already offering each home the riches collected in the greatest libraries and foremost research centers. Schools, universities, and cultural institutions are busy exploiting these opportunities, trying to integrate them progressively without upsetting educational and pedagogical objectives.

Apart from electronic communications, there are the communications provided by rapid transport. All the points of the globe have become amazingly close to us in time and space. Air travel in particular has established a more or less unified system of communications and relations between all the different countries. The concepts of "foreigner," "neighbor," and "traveler" have undergone a decided redimensioning in our minds. The human family has become closer and more present.

This phenomenon is transforming the Church itself in its style of communication, participation, information, presence, and evangelization. The geography of the Church is made up of a universal network that makes catholicity, co-responsibility, and collegiality immediately present, analogously calling to mind Péguy's reflection on the Roman legions opening up a new world for later missionaries: "The feet of the legions had marched for Him." Modern inventors are also opening up new paths for humanity as it waits for the Gospel.

### Toward a Superculture?

Our discernment with regard to these phenomena of universalizing communication is still extremely inadequate, and all the more so since the various forms of fallout from the media are far from being totally positive. One of the most notable effects is the birth of a mass culture brought about by the standardization of tastes, the universal spread of styles of life and consumption, and the increasing hold of cultural industries that know how to combine the creation of popular works with financial success.

This results in a homogenization of culture and a new form of dominance, which tends to be western and American, although not at all exclusively so, as we shall see. These leisure values, with their predominantly materialistic and hedonistic basis, seduce the masses, whose tastes tend to become more and more similar in every part of the world. This superculture is becoming progressively more universal and thus constitutes a threat to regional, national, ethnic, and religious cultures. The values relating to the family and traditional collectivities are undergoing an almost irresistible erosion. A number of cultural communities are in danger of disappearing; some are holding their own, while others are offering violent opposition, as can be seen in the revival of various types of nationalism but also of fundamentalism and religious fanaticism.

One of the most serious challenges facing our era is that of reconciling the advent of a superculture with the peaceful coexistence of particular cultures; that is, to consciously find an equilibrium between one homogeneous and universalized culture, already present, and the various living cultures that are now on the defensive. Such cultural internationalism is called for; it is made up of a respectful pluralism and has some realistic and farseeing supporters today. It represents a form of defense of the human being as such that cannot leave believers indifferent.

### Socialization of Evil

Another effect of the media that deserves in-depth reflection and joint cultural action is the phenomenon of the socialization of evil in the ethos of modern populations. The spirit of evil, crime, dishonesty, and malice was born with man as a sinner and has always been found in every society, giving rise to scandal and collective sanctions. However, never before has the *socialization* of moral disorder been so universal and omnipresent. Violence, brutality, criminality, hedonism, irreligiosity, and professed immorality are vast phenomena to which the whole of society and each individual, children as well as adults, are exposed. This banalization of disorder and destruction of moral values are leading to the degeneration of every culture that remains too passive.

Within the context of this cultural situation, the modern scourge of drug abuse has spread, especially among the young, becoming a very dangerous plague affecting all the industrialized countries, spreading throughout Eastern Europe and the developing countries. A worldwide system of production, distribution, and information has been able to spread a new set of behavior patterns — that of the drug consumer — throughout the world.

The most serious aspect is the involvement of vast investments on an international scale that prosper by spreading vice of various types: drugs, pornography, organized crime, prostitution, and entertainment pandering to depravity. Global tourism tends to exacerbate and spread these social problems. Advertising and the media broadly support the commercialization of immorality and the paganization of consciences. The media have unlimited and almost uncontrollable power. Immense interests are at stake here, and the profit motive tends all too often to become the sole rule guiding the producers of the media. Terrorists have understood this: without the media, they would be neutralized and reduced to silence.

### What Regulation for the Media?

Has mass culture, disseminated by the media, reached a limit beyond which it will in fact cause its own self-destruction? This is one of the most urgent and difficult moral and political questions that must be considered by those citizens anxious to ensure the survival of the fundamental institutions of modern society. We must overcome a great many obstacles, vested interests, conspiracies, and passivity, in order to come to grips with this enormous challenge, which affects the very future of culture.

In ancient times, people entrusted their security to guardians of the city, for without them there was no hope: *Quis custodiet custodes?* Today the question is still with us: "Who will guard the guardians?" Who will guarantee the protection and regulation of the most precious human territory, that of living cultures? The image and reality of the external enemy have not disappeared from the collective consciousness, but the present line of defense, the one that is undoubtedly more difficult to hold, is the interior. How are we to regulate the impact modern technologies have deep within the human soul? Legal coercion or censorship will not be adequate solutions. It is first through cultural means that a culture defends itself and its major values. Education, public awareness, and especially the creative use of the media, appear to be the proper response to this new challenge. We still have much to learn in this matter.

## SCIENCE, A CREATIVE AND THREATENING POWER

As we admitted, science and technology have been the driving forces in modernization, and the discoveries of scientific creativity have changed civilization forever. Nobody, except anti-scientific and anti-intellectual movements, can dream of some illusory return to a sort of pre-scientific and naturalistic society. Even so, we should understand the motives behind such nostalgia. The same technological science that was a triumphant hope and the true creator of marvels yesterday is under accusation by the universal conscience today. Its power has undergone almost unlimited growth, not only for our well-being, but also for the destruction of us and our habitat. There is no man or woman today who is not haunted by the murderous and suicidal capacities of modern arms. Hiroshima has made a lasting mark on the collective psyche. Cultures and civilizations are mortal, and they can all be wiped out by a cataclysm unleashed by a human hand.

Nature and the biosphere have already been seriously ravaged, and dramatic catastrophes such as Chernobyl in the Soviet Union, Bophal in India, Seveso in Italy, and the blazing oil wells in Kuwait give rise to a general anxiety that often borders on panic. The irrationalism of industrialized and militarized society leads to devastation. Serious studies provide us with alarming facts:

> The data are overwhelmingly clear in their import. Most devastating are those which show rates of soil erosion, desertification, deforestation, species loss, pollution, as well as the very fully documented facts on militarization, increasing violence, income disparity, human suffering, and wasted potential. Even if some estimates vary, most of them are more likely to be underestimates, rather than overestimates.[18]

The ecological and pacifist movements may be irritating because of their extremism, but their accusations are by and large based on well-founded facts. They offer a challenge to our cultures, which are too unconcerned and passive over the havoc wreaked by uncontrolled industrialization, and over military programs that should be condemned.

Has the sorcerer's apprentice lost control of his magic? The "scientific spirit" of our age has been deeply humiliated by major ecological catastrophes, by disastrous famine, and by the distressing impotence of medicine in the face of the ravages of AIDS. Despite this, hazardous experiments continue unabated. Human beings are being subjected to all kinds of genetic manipulation, as well as experiments with artificial insemination, cross-fertilization, and embryo engineering. Even now, governments are barely coming to grips with such problems and their very serious ethical and juridical implications. Our contemporaries are anxious and afraid of what the future holds. We would also observe that our social environment is under at least as great a threat as our physical environment.

### What about the Human Sciences?

The products of the human sciences are less visible than those of technology, but is their impact any less profound? When we consider science today, do we pay sufficient attention to the behavioral sciences? These disciplines have expanded our knowledge of human reality to a considerable degree and have enabled us to make remarkable advances in the psycho-social understanding of behavior and in the organization and management of human communities. The functioning of modern society would be inconceivable without the social sciences, and they are indispensable for the modernization of the world. However, there is a deterministic and structuralistic tendency to destroy the humanistic concept inherited from the Bible and the world of the Greeks and Romans. There are sociologists, economists, and political scientists disseminating a materialistic view of the human being. And when anthropologists and psychiatrists dismantle the workings of the unconscious and the hidden structures of behavior, they strip the human soul naked before the dark, anxiety-producing forces that inhabit it. Some people hold that human beings are simply miserable playthings at the mercy of their unconscious impulses. Claude Lévi-Strauss, whose works are known throughout the world, even stated that "the final aim of the human sciences is not that of building man up, but dissolving him,"[19] and this paradoxical statement brings us back to the need to reconstitute a new, postmodern humanism.

### Religion No Longer Functional?

Paul Ricoeur has devoted a great deal of study to these challenges that have been addressed to modern culture, especially to philosophy and theology. The legitimization of cultural institutions used to be provided by religion, but today "religion is no longer directly functional," either in the scientific sphere or in the ethical, political, and social spheres. In these circumstances what becomes of transcendence, the absolute, and religion? Were they simply constructions of the uncritical spirit? Ricoeur writes:

These scientifically justified observations force philosophers to examine the changing motivations of religion and the relations between ethics and religion. . . . Psychology, and especially psychoanalysis has carried the criticism of religion a very long way through examination of the motives that could have led people to be religious. . . . Psychoanalysis has shown the function that the absolute, omnipotence and knowledge can have in the economy of desires. Although through its own intelligibility psychoanalysis does not belong to the metaphysical order, in the mind of its founder it sought to replace metaphysics with metapsychology and offer a reductionist interpretation of all the concepts that go to make up the philosophy of the absolute.[20]

These observations give us a picture of the condition of contemporary people in their radical situation, raising the question of whether they are still capable of finding their existential place, in a psychologically significant relationship, with regard to the absolute and transcendence. Ricoeur warns that if they are not, humanism and culture will break down into nihilism.

## TOWARD THE SELF-DESTRUCTION OF MODERNITY?

A number of recent authors draw the conclusion that from now on modernity is heading for self-destruction. Progress will drive out progress and human culture. The frenetic race for novelty and superabundance, the search for ever more extravagant sensations, and change for the sake of change will end up by destroying modernity.

### Entering a Postmodern Era?

According to this view, modernity has exhausted its innovating dynamics and we are already in the postmodern era, in which history can be brought under control only by a concerted worldwide effort. History is no longer tutelary, as it was thought to be in the utopia of the nineteenth century. Historicism was destroyed by its false dreams. Each one of us is responsible for producing an intentional, humanized history, and all should participate in its construction. Otherwise, the crushing hegemony of uncontrolled technology and the media will bring on the death throes of humanity and the extinction of civilization. Many think that we are already entering a new barbarian age. A number of observers firmly support this view, expressing it in analyses that are deeply disturbing, even though they should not lead us to abandon all hope so soon.

At the beginning of the century, Spengler set himself up as a prophet of doom and foretold the inexorable decline of the West. History has proved much more complex. On the one hand, the West has continued its forward movement, and on the other, Spengler did not foresee that modernity would not be identified exclusively with the western world for very long.

Modernization first arose in Europe, but it soon spread to the United States, which in turn became its main exponent, until in due course the leadership became polycentric. Japan in particular has astonished the whole world with its technical creativity and the cultural impact of its products. The disintegration of the Soviet Union should not hide the fact that it was entering the scientific and industrial game; its military buildup and its space ventures revealed its astonishing power, which is now potentially spread among the independent Republics. The European Economic Community is a fast-growing giant which is changing the geography of world competition. Brazil and India are respectable industrial powers, and Indian studios produce the highest number of films in the world. The nations of southeast Asia are rocking trade, financial dealings, and human relations in the Pacific area, and their influence is felt internationally.

### Is Modernity Still a Western Phenomenon?

We must then consider the extent to which modernity is still a western, and predominantly American, phenomenon. A clear cultural internationalization has taken place, and modernity is tending to become a culture common to all those peoples who have accepted industrialization as a way of life. Kenneth Boulding observed this transnationalization of modernity:

> The *superculture* is the culture of airports, superhighways, skyscrapers, hybrid varieties of maize, artificial fertilizers,

the pill, and universities. Its sphere of action is universal, and, in a very real sense too, all the airports are the same airport, and all the universities are the same university. It even has its own universal language, technical English, and a common ideology, that of science.[21]

In the fifties, American philosopher Hannah Arendt addressed the following words of warning to Europe: "In actual fact, what Europeans fear under the name of Americanization is simply the advent of the modern world with all its perplexities and implications."[22] Professor Gregory Claeys of Hanover subscribes to the same view.

> It seemed clearer and clearer towards the beginning of the 1960s — and how satisfying it is to recognize this today — that the transformation of Europe in the post-war period in fact had much less to do with Americanization than with the spread of a new style of consumption and new forms of production and distribution characteristic of a specific stage in the evolution of industrial society.[23]

### Modernity and Non-European Values

At a deeper level, we have to recognize that the cultures of the non-European world have shaken the self-centered ideologies of the West. Mircea Eliade saw that coming in the 1950s: "The major phenomenon of the 20th century has not been, and indeed will not be, the revolution of the proletariat . . . but the discovery of the non-European man and his spiritual universe."[24]

The great world religions, their heritage as well as their challenges to the new world order, are now part of our modern psychology. The cultural revolution of Islam and the confrontation of all traditional religions with the technical age are giving new dimensions to the common conscience of our era. Modernity has become a major concern for all cultures and all spiritual families. The future of humanity and its peaceful development is now better understood as a moral and spiritual problem. This was made manifest by the remarkable meeting in Assisi on October 27, 1986, where representatives of the great religions of the world met with John Paul II and prayed for peace. This is one of the promising signs of the new times.

### Poor Countries and Modernity

If we accept that modernity has been identified first with the industrially richer countries, we must face the unavoidable question of what will happen to the poorer countries. It must be admitted that the modern world has not been very successful in dealing with the problems of development. Despite considerable and often generous efforts, the numbers of the poor, the illiterate, and the hungry in the world continue to grow, and this constitutes a dramatic failure for modern culture, which has been unable to mobilize the resources and commitment that could have ensured the social and economic take-off of the whole community of nations. The technical means, capital, and expertise do exist, but they have not been put into operation with a clear-sighted will. During the same period, fabulous sums and unlimited efforts have been poured into the militarization of our planet — and this applies to poor countries as well as rich ones — so that we have now reached a suicidal saturation point. Statistics show that over half the people engaged in research today are working on projects connected with war. Even a minute percentage of these efforts could have produced extraordinary results in the task of overall development of the earth.

Although this contradiction undoubtedly reveals the most tragic disease of modern culture, modernity should not in itself be condemned. Despite a great many setbacks and errors, we must hope for a moral upsurge in every nation, both rich and poor. Our era is called to a cultural conversion to mobilize the human energies and effective means that will finally be capable of fostering the forms of solidarity indispensable for the development of all peoples, to be carried out in a concerted effort with all those involved on a worldwide scale. We should not lose sight of the fact that as an ideal project, modernization still nourishes the dreams and legitimate hopes of every man and woman, even the most destitute. What form shall we give to modernity, which will one day undoubtedly reach the whole human family?

*A Challenge to Christians*

Throughout the foregoing analysis, we could perceive the serious problems that modernity is presenting the Church. We are only at the beginning of a long and complex task of inculturation of the faith into societies characterized by the modern spirit. In this last section we shall try less to provide answers, which still need to mature further in a joint interdisciplinary effort, than to describe some attitudes resulting from a reflection on the inculturation of the faith into modernity. The Church itself will have much to gain in its creative relationship with modern culture.

Let us recall that inculturation implies a reciprocity and mutual enrichment of persons and groups in the encounter of the Gospel with contemporary society.[25]

Taking this into consideration, the inculturation of the Gospel in modern society will require on the part of the evangelizer: 1) a receptive attitude and critical discernment; 2) the capacity to perceive the spiritual expectations and human aspirations of new cultures; 3) the aptitude for cultural analysis leading to cultural action.

## COMBINING RESEARCH AND ACTION

### ATTITUDE OF APPRECIATION AND DISCERNMENT

An attitude of appreciation is the first thing needed by any person who wants to understand and evangelize the contemporary world. As we have seen, modernity is accompanied by undeniable advances in the material and cultural spheres: improved well-being, human mobility, science, research, education, and a new sense of human solidarity. At Vatican II, the Church took a courageous position with relation to the contemporary world, and the Church of tomorrow will be built within the cultures of modernity.

It is not easy for everybody to practice this attitude of acceptance. The weight of the past and acquired habits act as a brake on this movement, aggravated by the fact that a good number of believers persist in viewing modernity as setting itself up in opposition to the Church through the secularization of mentalities and the rejection of spiritual traditions. The official opposition of the nineteenth-century Church to "modern civilization" still lives on in some minds. They forget that what Pius IX condemned was the liberalism of his day, with its anti-Christian conception of modernity.[26] Such an attitude of simply identifying liberalism and modernity is anachronistic today and is indefensible in the case of those who want to Christianize contemporary cultures. The Church calls us, rather, to adopt an approach of *critical discernment* of modernity.

### Whatever May Be Reconciled with the Gospel

The same yardstick is valid for modern culture as for traditional cultures; it is the one that has been repeated many times in Catholic missionary teaching, from Pius X down to our own day. In *Summi Pontificatus* (1939), for example, Pius XII expresses the principle as follows:

> We must follow the very prudent norm that when peoples embrace the Gospel message, we should not ruin or destroy anything good, decent, and beautiful in their own character and native spirit. Everything in the customs of peoples that is not inextricably bound up with superstition or error should be examined favorably and, if possible, preserved intact.[27]

In our earlier discussion we emphasized the ways in which modern civilization has undeniably enriched the Church, improving its mobility, methods of communication, and government, and also its knowledge of the physical universe and of the human being. Maybe we do not sufficiently appreciate this contribution of modernity to the growth of the Church.

### Becoming Cultural Critics

Such appreciation obviously should not blind us to the negative values of present societies, and we need a critical spirit in order to speak out against everything in modern culture that is contrary to the Gospel and human dignity. This is not an easy task, inasmuch as a great deal of courage and clear thinking is needed in order to criticize one's own culture, because of the extent to which we are personally identified with the ways of life accepted as normal by our contemporaries. We are unconsciously touched by the spirit of our times and by the consumer habits, hedonism, secularization, and ethnocentrism of the society around us. It is very difficult to have enough detachment to weigh up the values and countervalues of our own culture. Many people are handicapped by a sort of cultural chauvinism, which is presently challenged by the increasing mobility of populations and the pressure of the new immigrants who are giving our major urban centers a cosmopolitan look and a new cultural profile.

## PERCEIVING THE EXPECTATIONS AND HOPES OF CULTURES

What we must try to discern are the states of mind found in a society living the experience of modernity. A methodical assessment has to be promoted as a joint effort in the whole Church. Looking into the cultural profile of people will reveal their spiritual longings and needs, their fragility and hopes. More or less consciously, the collective soul is manifesting new religious dimensions. We are stuck today by certain psychosocial features of great spiritual relevance, which we can attempt to describe in summary form as follows.

### Fear and Anxiety

A feeling of fear and anxiety with regard to the future seems to be developing, and this is especially true of the past twenty years. There is an increasingly generalized, dull uneasiness over the destruction of nature and the environment, the unpredictable consequences of biological experiments, the spreading conflict between ethnic groups, and the overwhelming dangers of a nuclear apocalypse. These anxieties remind us sharply of our collective responsibility. Never before have human beings as a group been so sensitive to the great original commandments found in the first pages of Genesis. We must take God's word seriously when we are made guardians of creation and of our fellow human beings.

The feeling of existential anxiety about the future brings us all back to an elementary philosophy and a radical search for human survival. We are called to show mercy toward this generation, which feels so seriously threatened in its very humanity. We are facing a real ontological crisis, one that is experienced as such by people today. It is no longer simply a crisis of morals or a crisis of atheism or agnosticism; what is at stake here is the human being as such. The religious distress spoken of by the young Marx is no longer confined to the proleteriat, but affects all classes or categories that make up modern society. There is today, especially among the young, an immense thirst and search for meaning and for ultimate motivations. We must learn to present the hope of the Gospel within this psycho-social setting. Christ will be seen as the true Liberator who rescues us from our moral powerlessness. God is not far away from those who suffer and admit their distress. We should recognize a pre-evangelization condition in such a state of mind.

### Overcoming Fatalism

The great temptation of our times is fatalism and the feeling of powerlessness in the face of infinitely complex problems that are greater than all of us. Christians reject this temptation to resignation, this tragic determinism that paralyzes too many minds. Believers should be the first to proclaim the firm conviction that the world can in fact regain control of its future by a moral and spiritual upsurge. The Gospel can teach the interdependent society of today that a joint effort to build up a humanized culture is truly possible. In its universality, the Church undoubtedly has a major role to play in this task of bringing about a modern culture in which responsibility is shared jointly. Powerful yearnings can help us in this effort at evangelization. Many examples come to mind.

**Justice and Peace.** The universal search for justice and peace has been strongly expressed in recent times. When people today discover their close interdependence, they find it increasingly difficult to accept the coexistence of extreme poverty and ostentatious affluence. A universal aspiration is arising in the world for a principle of unity, justice, and co-responsibility, encompassing freedom and respect for all. A sort of cultural catholicity is coming into being, and it represents a hope that should definitely be explored. More than ever before, the defense of human rights is seen as a requirement and a sign of the liberation brought by Christ. Today there are vast masses who cannot bear any longer the refusal of their fundamental liberties, their right to development, and above all their freedom of conscience and religion. This might be called the revolution of hope. We all come to realize that the development of the human family is feasible and depends essentially on a generalized attitude of solidarity. This is a sign of the times, and it is really a preparation for evangelization.

**New Cultures.** The rise of new cultures offers another aspect for reflection and Christian commitment. Do we pay enough attention to the values that are being sought, especially by the younger generations and the newer nations? Let us try to understand the expectations expressed through such values as respect for one's identity, the quality of life, access to education, culture, and communication, the new role of women, re-evaluation of work and free time, the search for community life, new interest in religion, new understanding of tolerance and pluralism, rediscovery of the family, dialogue between generations, concern for the handicapped, and the universal yearning for peace and solidarity. Special attention and discernment must be devoted to the very striking search for religious experiences that is seen as a new need in a wide variety of circles, particularly among the young.

A special place among the new values is occupied by an increased awareness of the fact that each person has his or her own dignity and rights and can legitimately aspire to free participation in the affairs of the community. Maybe we should see this as the latent hope of individuals and societies to embrace the Gospel ideal of brotherhood.

Such cultural tendencies can sometimes be ambiguous in form, but they do convey deep human expectations. We should strive to purify them and help them develop into Christian hope.

**Men and Women.** The new relationship between men and women represents another cultural turning point of historic importance. It is not simply a movement for the assertion of rights, although even as such it has been recognized far too late by many Catholics. We are dealing, rather, with the promotion of a new condition for women within modern society. A new balance between female and male is being sought throughout the whole human family. This cultural challenge is now more clearly understood in its complexity and ramifications. If women acquire equal freedom and responsibility in society, the result is human progress that will benefit all humankind. In this perspective, men, just as much as women, are called to be the subjects and agents of change in female roles. In other words, both men and women must grow together in their necessary and indissoluble complementarity. This evolution will affect human beings, as such, and represents one of the deepest cultural changes that the modern world has known. Christians must redefine the first words of the Bible for our age: "In the image of God he created Man; male and female he created them." We are only at the beginning of this cultural evolution in which Christian values have a vital service to offer human beings, as such.

**Signs of Contradiction.** From the more specifically evangelical point of view, we have to consider some fundamental questions when we see the behavior of modern men and women. How can we make human beings understand the radical message of Jesus? Are we still capable of accepting the supreme words and the meaning of *charity*, *evangelical poverty*, and *adoration* of the Father? Have we paid enough attention to the fact that modern culture has wiped its psychological horizon clean of human suffering, and especially death, which is an unmentionable event, hidden from the public gaze in our societies? How are we to teach our brothers and sisters today that, in St. Paul's words, "Death spread to all because all sinned" (Rom. 5:12)? It is on this level of the collective spirit that inculturation is most difficult, but also most necessary: How are we to foster an attitude of faith and hope in the work of Resurrection wrought by the risen Christ? This is why inculturation resists any utopian and facile effort to spread the Gospel among the masses. Christ remains a "sign of contradiction." The Gospel will never be a dominating ideology, and especially not in a pluralistic society. Evangelizaton of culture is directed to the human person, in order to come back to other persons, whose destiny is that of "working first for the kingdom of heaven."

## CULTURAL ANALYSIS LEADING TO CULTURAL ACTION

We therefore recognize our obligation to develop a capacity to analyze cultures, both in themselves and in their moral and spiritual significance. Is the church properly equipped to carry out this task of methodical investigation and apostolic discernment? Some very praiseworthy efforts are being carried out in research centers and among Christian groups, but we are still only at the beginning, since, as we have seen, modernity is a very ambivalent and complex phenomenon to grasp and interpret in the perspective of collective psychologies and Christian concerns. Priests, religious men and women, and the Christian laity seldom receive any training that would enable them to analyze living cultures. In their college training, they are taught to read, understand, and analyze the classical texts, major authors, and scientific writings, but they are hardly provided with even the rudiments of reading and analyzing living cultures in their human, moral, and spiritual dimensions.

### Reconciling the Two Faces of Culture

Our discussions on the future of modernity invite us to further reflection and joint research in an ecumenical spirit and in cooperation with all persons of good will.What we see more clearly, I think, is that we have to broaden our usual way of trying to influence cultures. In general, we are more at ease when we deal with the intellectual and aesthetic side of culture. We are more familiar with the method of influencing cultures through ideas, scientific invention, and artistic creativity. Our traditional intellectual approach still retains all its validity, of course, since ideas and philosophies do make a difference and do change cultures. Analyzing philosophical systems and their influence on society remains indispensable, but we see more clearly today the urgency of studying cultures as specific realities generating new ways of living, thinking, behaving. A different and complementary approach is now revealing itself as necessary.

In other words, we are becoming more sensitive today to the anthropological side of cultures, which are influenced not only by intellectual thought but also by the revolution of values, sentiments, and mentalities. Cultures are profoundly transformed in modern society by the human impact of industrialization, urbanization, mass communications, global interdependence, and the universal hope for a just world. This being so, our cultural action must take on a new dimension. We must try to analyze the dominant life-styles around us, criticizing them and finding new ways to act on the key values that give form to cultures.

Of course, our action will predominantly remain on the educational level, in training minds and consciences, but we must also teach the young generations that the culture of tomorrow depends on their common discernment, joint effort, and ability to mold cultural reality, as such.

### Impossible Mission?

Many might think that evangelizing the culture of modernity is an impossible task. It seems utopian to try to convert a culture marked by pluralism, secularization, and the privatization of all creeds. Indeed the task appears beyond human reach. Yet more than once throughout history, Christians have succeeded in implanting the Gospel values in the cultures of their times, transforming the mentalities not only of the poor and uneducated, but also of thinkers, philosophers, artists, and rulers of nations. The regenerative power of the Gospel remains as promising today as in the past. It depends on us to show how the Gospel can become a ferment changing mentalities and lifestyles. That persuasion has been alive in Christians since the beginning and has accompanied them ever since.

A great historian of Christianity, Henri-Irénée Marrou, from the Sorbonne, has well analyzed this surprising creativity of the believers in Christ and their almost exorbitant hope of transforming cultures. Marrou points to "the omnipotence of a resolute minority" convinced of being, as it were, the "soul of the world." He writes boldly:

> So it is, we Christians alone, however unworthy and few in number, who can and must take on responsibility for the world and the direction of history. We alone can give it meaning, implant it within metaphysical reality. I shall quote here the mysterious words which an unknown apologist flung at a pagan world in the second century: "Suffice it to say that what the soul is to the body, Christians are to the world."[28]

These are strong expressions, indeed, and certainly unacceptable to many, today as yesterday, who would accuse Christians of professing an idealogy of worldly domination, but not unacceptable to those of us who are convinced that the Gospel can enlighten the cultures of the new times, as it did in the past. That was, in fact, the persuasion of Saint Augustine, witnessing the end of ancient culture and laying the foundation for the new times. The whole history of civilization after Christ is marked by the leading role of great thinkers, writers, and saints whose impact was determinant on the cultures of their times: Origen, St. Cyril and St. Methodius, St. Irenaeus, St. Benedict, St. Thomas Aquinas, St. Catherine of Siena, St. Dominic, St. Francis and St. Clare of Assisi, St. Teresa of Avila, St. Ignatius of Loyola.

If we admit that the act of faith is the highest accomplishment of the human person, then we understand how faith is capable of creating culture. In fact, our faith would remain superficial and rootless if it did not pervade our culture. A synthesis between faith and culture is then called for, as John Paul II puts it: "The synthesis between culture and faith is not just a demand of culture, but also of faith. . . . A faith which does not become culture is a faith which has not been fully received, not thoroughly thought through, not faithfully lived out."[29]

In short, we have to discover—intellectually and spiritually—how the Gospel of Christ can be conveyed to persons as well as to the living cultures of modern society. After Vatican II, the Church has strongly committed itself to this vital mission, as John Paul II reminds us constantly:

> It is in the name of the Christian faith that the Second Vatican Council committed the whole Church to listen to modern men and women in order to understand them and to invent a new kind of dialogue which would permit the originality of the Gospel message to be carried to the heart of contemporary mentalities. We must then rediscover the apostolic creativity and the prophetic power of the first disciples in order to face new cultures. Christ's word must appear in all of its freshness to the young generations whose attitudes are sometimes so difficult to understand for the traditionally-minded, but who are far from being closed to spiritual values.[30]

# 3

# Inculturation: A Modern Approach to Evangelization

*Inculturation* is a new term in the official language of the Church. The documents of Vatican II did not use the word. John Paul II is the first Pope to speak explicitly of inculturation, and for him it has become a common expression. When new words start circulating, they usually point to new ways of seeing reality. In the case of *inculturation*, the word reveals a fresh approach to the evangelization of cultures. In this chapter, I would like to discuss this new approach to evangelization. While underlining the novelty of this approach, it is useful to explain it with two preliminary remarks. First, the word *inculturation*, although recent in official Church language, has been in use for over fifty years among Catholics. Second, the objective of inculturation — the penetration of the Gospel in cultures — is as old as the history of evangelization and was taking place long before the recent formulation of a new method of inculturation. These traditional and innovative aspects of inculturation deserve close attention.[1]

## TRADITIONAL AND INNOVATIVE CHARACTER OF INCULTURATION

### TRADITIONAL ASPECTS

Since its inception, the Church's mission has taken the form of a mutually enriching encounter between evangelizers and cultures. St. Paul made Christ's message accessible to Greeks and other Gentiles, and the Gospel message was soon proclaimed in Rome and all the areas of the Roman Empire. Thanks to the Apostles and their first successors, the Gospel of Christ was announced in the Middle East, in Europe, and as far as India, marking all those cultures lastingly. In later centuries, theologians of genius, such as Origen and Augustine, sought to express the essentials of Jesus' message in the thought categories of the main cultures of their age. The whole history of missions embodies an effort to adapt evangelization to the different languages, customs and traditions of the countries that were to be evangelized, so the effort to accommodate or interpret the Gospel message in terms intelligible to every culture is not something new; it fits right in with Christ's own teaching, which was addressed "to all nations."

The great encyclicals on the missions published in this century[2] have described the historical experience of the Church in evangelizing peoples and cultures and have proposed original methods that need to be examined in regard to inculturation. Let me recall, for instance, the two basic principles formulated by Pius XII that have become guiding norms for the evangelization of cultures: "We must follow the very prudent norm that when peoples embrace the Gospel message, we should not ruin or destroy anything good, decent, and beautiful in their own character and native spirit."

"Everything in the customs of peoples that is not inextricably bound up with superstition or error should be examined favorably and, if possible, preserved intact."[3]

PRESENT RELEVANCE

Today, inculturation is seen in a new perspective. The main reason for this is that the Church, especially after Vatican II, has become much more conscious of the necessity to pursue explicitly the evangelization of cultures as such, in a methodical and concerted way. Catholics now perceive cultures with new eyes, discovering in them aspirations, spiritual needs, secret hopes, and the need to be redeemed. A new dialogue has been initiated between the Church and cultures. For reasons we shall

be examining further on, the Church's encounter with cultures
is now posing new problems and arousing new interest. Progress
in theology and the social sciences has enabled us to get a
sharper focus on the crucial issue of inculturation and explore
it more deeply.

The present-day relevance of the problem of inculturation
for the Church is due mainly to the fact that cultural interchanges have greatly intensified in our age, provoking confron-
tations between cultures and the defense of the cultural identity
of each people. *Identity* becomes a key value in all cultures
undergoing rapid change. The period of decolonization after
World War II entailed a broad movement for "cultural liberation" and criticism of cultural dependence. In the young
churches of Africa and Asia, in particular, we see a historical
reexamination of the evangelization effected by Westerners.
They certainly managed to proclaim the Good News and implant
the Church, but they did not always succeed in touching the
innermost depths of native cultures. There has also been criticism of the methods of evangelization. Some critics do not hesitate to say that the attitude of missionaries, seen from a *cultural
standpoint*, was not wholly unlike that of the colonizers, admin-
istrators, and merchants who came to the new territories and
transplanted there the values, institutions, languages, practices,
and ways of thinking of their mother countries. Missionaries did
announce Jesus Christ, but they kept thinking and operating
within the cultural framework of their homelands.

At the time of decolonization, Asian and African theologians,
and many Westerners as well, posed the issue of inculturation
with new urgency. In particular, they wondered why indigenous
cultures had not been radically converted by Christian values in
many instances, why a substratum of traditional beliefs continued to persist. On the other hand, missionaries had not always
managed to perceive the religious significance of certain local
customs. Theologians began asking how Christianity could
become more deeply inculturated in various cultures whose specific characters were becoming better known and appreciated.
They talked of stripping Christianity of its western cultural dress
in order to effect a real Indianization, Africanization, or indigenization of autochthonous Churches.

Debate about inculturation was not confined to the pastoral methods of the Church. It also dealt with the language of theology, moral teaching, Church law and liturgical expression. Some questioners went even further and wondered how the Church might be able to welcome into its own inner life worthwhile elements of ancestral beliefs and ethical values espoused by traditional religions, perhaps even adopting their sacred texts. The seriousness and complexity of the questions raised in this debate pointed out the need for deeper studies of a systematic and interdisciplinary nature, studies that would respect both theological principles and serious anthropological analysis.

A more recent development is the realization that inculturation does not concern only the so-called mission lands, but also the countries of Christian tradition, where a secularized culture requires a second evangelization. The culture of modernity is itself in need of evangelization, and this now concerns all countries touched by industrialization and urbanization. An urgent need is felt everywhere to define better what inculturation really means and to determine some guiding criteria for the indispensable and complex task of inculturation.[4]

## WORKING DESCRIPTION OF INCULTURATION

### BRIEF FORMULATION

Let us try to formulate a working description of inculturation as it is generally conceived by Catholics. From the standpoint of the evangelizer, inculturation is the effort to inject Christ's message into a given socio-cultural milieu, thereby summoning that milieu to grow in accordance with its own values, so long as they can be reconciled with the Gospel message. Inculturation seeks to naturalize the Church in every country, region, and social sector, while fully respecting the native genius and character of each human collectivity. Thus, the term *inculturation* includes the notions of growth and mutual enrichment for the persons and groups involved in the encounter of the Gospel message with a social milieu.[5]

Inculturation applies first to individuals, groups, and institutions that incorporate Gospel values. By extension it also applies to the mentalities, customs, forms of expression, values, and practices that the work of evangelization is trying to inspire. Later on, I shall add further specifications and details to this preliminary description of inculturation. The phenomenon or concept of inculturation does not signify an entirely new reality, but present-day happenings do give it a certain novelty: a new sensitivity regarding cultures and a new, methodic, and concerted effort to evangelize them.

## INCULTURATION AND ACCULTURATION

The term *inculturation* is related to the term *acculturation*. The latter term was first used by anthropologists around the end of the last century; then it came to be used by German and other European anthropologists.[6] The concept of acculturation has also been employed for a long time by Catholics in studying the relationship between the Gospel message and traditional or modern cultures. It is still used by Catholics; sometimes it serves as a synonym for inculturation, as certain discourses of John Paul II indicate.[7] But the tendency today is to make a distinction between inculturation and acculturation, in order to make clear that relationships between the Gospel message and culture are not reducible to mere relationships between cultures (i.e., acculturation). We are dealing specifically with the encounter of the Christian message with cultures, and the term *inculturation* suggests an analogy with the term *incarnation*.

The concept of inculturation cannot be strictly defined in a simple formula. It refers to very complex realities—Christian message and cultures—entering into a living relationship. The nature of this process is the object of much continuing research by theologians and sociologists. Here our aim is to understand the many dimensions of inculturation as it applies to the pastoral mission of the Church and to the practice of evangelization. We will see that the task of inculturation presupposes some fundamental conditions: first of all, a clear vision that culture is a proper field of evangelization; second, that the encounter between faith and culture should respect some anthropological and theological requirements. Let us begin with the key condition of all inculturation: the conviction that cultures can effectively be evangelized.

## THE FUNDAMENTAL GOAL: EVANGELIZE CULTURES

### CULTURE SEEN AS AN AREA OF EVANGELIZATION

In the first place, Christians must have a mental perception of culture as a human reality to be evangelized; they must also be capable of "listening to modern men and women in order to understand them and invent a new kind of dialogue capable of carrying the originality of the Gospel message into the very heart of present-day mentalities."[8] In other words, they must perceive mentalities—collective attitudes—as a specific field for evangelization.

Evangelization must be understood in its full individual and societal sense. It is certainly true that only persons can make the act of faith, undergo conversion, receive Baptism and other sacraments, contemplate and worship God. But it is equally true that evangelization can transform cultures through persons acting as intermediaries. "We must evangelize—not in a superficial or merely decorative sense but in an in-depth way that goes to the roots—human culture and human cultures, understanding those terms in the broad, rich sense given them in *Gaudium et Spes*, always starting from the person and always returning to the relationship of persons with each other and with God."[9] Persons will bring the light of the Gospel in their milieu, starting with the family, which is a primary agent of evangelization.[10]

Christians today are beginning to realize better that culture has become a proper field for evangelization. Vast cultural fields have never accepted or rejected the light of the Gospel message. Respecting all human liberties but feeling the urgings of their faith, Christians now sense the urgency of proclaiming the Good News to today's world. As John Paul II put it: "We cannot not evangelize. Countless regions and cultural milieus remain unaware of the Good News of Jesus Christ. I am thinking of cultures in vast areas of the world that remain on the margins of the Christian faith. But I also have in mind vast cultural areas in traditionally Christian countries that today seem indifferent, if not resistant, to the Gospel message."[11] The Christian message produces its effect mainly on the level of the values — or preferred choices — that characterize a culture and give it an ethical sense.

## DISCERNING ETHICAL ORIENTATIONS

The evangelizer must grasp exactly which cultural values are capable of being enriched, purified, and perfected by the power of the Gospel message. Every culture has tendencies and aspirations of its own that we must try to discover and explore in terms of their ethical and spiritual dimensions. To put it more concretely, we must see how the Gospel message can purify and enrich those dimensions of a culture having to do with collective thinking and doing. The evangelizer has to discern the typical behavior patterns of a milieu; the dominant values and major interests; the habits and customs that leave their mark on work, leisure, and the practice of family, social, economic, and political life.

As we can readily see, all these elements belonging to what is known as the *ethos* of a culture can be appreciated, evaluated, and given direction in the light of the Gospel message. The ethos reveals the scale of values that gives more or less conscious direction to the behavior of a group. These codes of conduct, it should be noted, may not necessarily conform to the imperatives of objective morality. For example, a culture might regard as "normal" the superiority of one particular race, slavery, polygamy, infanticide, or abortion. Thus the ethos leaves room for moral and spiritual progress on the level of individual and group conduct.

In large measure, then, evangelizing means detecting, criticizing, and even denouncing the aspects of a culture that contradict the Gospel message and represent an attack on the dignity of the human being. For their part, Christians are convinced that their faith can have a real impact on every sector of individual and collective life. While fully respecting the autonomy of terrestrial realities, they must also testify that the spirit of the Gospel message really can transform individual behavior and the ethos of a society. To deny that would be to disavow the innovative power of the Gospel message as revealed by the history of the Church.

## CHRISTIANIZING CULTURAL PATTERNS

Evangelizers know, out of experience, that faith can really change the mind, conscience, and heart of human beings, bringing about new ways of thinking, feeling, and behaving in persons and in the whole society. New cultural patterns are thus inspired by Christian faith, and the Gospel becomes a ferment, changing mentalities and life-styles.

For some people, the notion of evangelizing cultures might seem difficult to understand or be construed as forced proselytism. We have to explain what we mean when we say that the Gospel can enrich cultures. We have to show concretely that, for those who believe in Christ, there is a Christian way of life that constitutes a new attitude and a new culture. It consists in a *particular way* of working, of resting, of celebrating joys and experiencing sorrows, of practicing business and politics, of managing an enterprise or a labor union, of using the media and publicity, of living family life, of loving one's spouse and educating children, of caring for the sick or running a hospital, of directing a school or a university, of defending human rights and helping the poor, of criticizing inhuman or degrading trends in the society. This is, in fact, what is meant by infusing Christian values in a living culture, by making the Gospel permeate the models of behavior that constitute a culture. A symbiosis of cultural values and faith values takes place: "The synthesis of culture and faith is not just an exigency of culture but an exigency of faith as well. A faith that does not become culture is a faith that is not fully accepted, completely thought out, and truly lived."[12]

Evangelization, however, is not to be equated with the production of a culture or the creation of a civilization. Pius XI noted this fact decades ago: "We must never lose sight of the fact that the aim of the Church is to evangelize, not to civilize. If the Church civilizes, it does so through evangelization."[13] Evangelization operates more like a leaven within any culture that accepts the Christian message, the latter transforming specific cultural traits.

A passage of Paul VI's *Evangelii Nuntiandi* well sums up the task of evangelizing cultures:

> For the church it is not simply a matter of preaching the Gospel message in ever wider geographical areas or to ever larger populations. It is also a matter of reaching and overturning, by the force of the Gospel message, the criteria of judgment, the ruling values, the points of interest, the lines of thinking, the sources of inspiration, and the patterns of living among human beings that are contrary to God's message and salvation plan.[14]

### Promoting a Culture of Justice

Thanks to Vatican II and its teachings, we have a better understanding of the different forms taken by the Church's work of evangelizing. We realize there are many different ministries and functions, due to the diversity of charisms. The mission of the Church is certainly carried out by the witness of faith in Jesus Christ, by prayer, contemplation, liturgical worship, preaching, and catechesis. Depending on circumstances, it can also take the form of dialogue with other believers, "to journey forward together in search of the truth and to cooperate in works of common interest." That would also include active commitment to the defense and betterment of the human being, both individual and social: a "real commitment to the service of human beings as well as any activity for societal improvement or against poverty and the structures that sustain it."[15] Let us remember this important point: in a broader sense than the one we examined earlier, the Church's work of evangelization is also carried out on the level of the defense of the human being and human rights. Much can be accomplished for justice and peace in cooperating more closely with believers of other religions.[16]

Do we Christians think enough of evangelization in terms of promoting a more human and just world? Are we really convinced that faith, hope, and charity can change the world? This is the plea made by John Paul II, especially in his encyclicals

*Sollicitudo Rei Socialis* and *Centesimus Annus*.[17] The social teaching of the Church is inseparable from her task of evangelization, as he has often repeated: "her social doctrine pertains to the Church's evangelizing mission and is an essential part of the Christian message." The new evangelization of today's cultures must therefore "include among its essential elements a proclamation of the Church's social doctrine." We should all feel responsible for the building of a world founded on ethical and cultural values. Our Christian outlook, of course, is not forced on the others, but we think that there are many in the world — persons and groups among believers and nonbelievers — who are ready to go along with our ideal of brotherhood, dignity, and justice for all. John Paul II said clearly: "The Church respects all cultures and imposes on no one her faith in Jesus Christ, but she invites all people of good will to promote a true civilization of love, founded on the evangelical values of brotherhood, justice and dignity for all."[18] When Christians join with other believers or persons of good will in serving human beings and their cultures, they perform an evangelizing action, insofar as the Gospel value concerning humanity and its dignity are defended and promoted. This aspect of Christian cultural action takes on considerable importance in an increasingly diversified and pluralistic world.

## GUIDELINES FOR INCULTURATION

Inculturation is then seen as a process through which the Church and cultures enter into a living relationship. This process should therefore follow the requirements governing these two orders of reality: *faith* and *cultures*. The following criteria appear particularly important.

### DISTINGUISH FAITH'S PROPER ROLE

The power of God's word can penetrate and elevate all human cultures, but we must maintain the radical distinction between the Gospel message and any culture. In other words, faith in Christ is not the product of any culture; its origin lies in a divine revelation. Furthermore, the Christian faith cannot

be identified exclusively with any historical culture; such an identification would mean its dissolution. The core of the Christian
message surpasses and transcends every culture, because it has
to do with the revelation of the mystery of the incarnate and
crucified God.[19] St. Paul himself preached the radical distinction
between this truth of faith and the cultures of his own day, the
latter seeing only scandal or folly in his proclamation of the
crucified Christ: "Jews demand signs and Greeks look for wisdom. But we preach Christ crucified, a stumbling block to Jews
and an absurdity to Gentiles."[20]

John XXIII stated that it would be a mistake to identify the
historical Church with Mediterranean culture, even though the
Church saw the light of day there. "The Church does not identify
itself with any one culture, not even with Western culture, to
which it is linked by its history."[21] Europe had a decisive role in
evangelizing the world, but its own experience of inculturation
does not constitute a unique model.[22]

The independence of the Gospel message from any and every
culture is ultimately rooted in the mystery of the Incarnation
which, historically speaking, also includes the Crucifixion and
the Resurrection. Here we are dealing with *divine facts* that
transcend every civilization and every culture. It is in this context
that we must grasp the exigency of inculturation for the Church.
As John Paul II told the Biblical Commission: "The term 'acculturation' or 'inculturation' may well be new, but it perfectly
expresses one of the elements of the great mystery of the Incarnation."[23] In one sense, inculturation prolongs the Incarnation
within the history of human peoples.

Paul VI spelled out the twofold principle that must be maintained in the process of inculturation. First, "the Gospel message and therefore evangelization are not at all identified with
culture. They are independent vis-à-vis all cultures." But once
we have asserted this principle of *distinction*, we must not think
that between the Gospel message and cultures there is nothing
but separation or dissociation. If that were the case, the Gospel
message could not possibly inspire cultures and transform them
from within, as it has in fact done for two thousand years. Christ
himself lived in a particular culture, and throughout its history
the Church has become incarnate in specific socio-cultural

milieus. Moreover, notes Paul VI, the Gospel message is lived by human beings who are linked to their own cultures. And he adds: "The building of the Kingdom of God cannot help but make use of cultural elements and human cultures. Although they are independent of cultures, the Gospel message and evangelization are not necessarily incompatible with them; rather, they are capable of impregnating all cultures without becoming enslaved to any."[24]

In fact, culture has a dynamic role to play in the process of redemption, as shown in the cultural experience of the Chosen People and of Christ himself, whose incarnation has also been "a cultural incarnation." John Paul II urges us not to consider culture "only from a passive angle" in the history of salvation. "Culture is not only a subject of redemption and elevation; it can also play a role of mediation and collaboration. In fact, God, in revealing Himself to the Chosen People, has used a particular culture. Jesus Christ, the Son of God, did the same: his human incarnation has also been a cultural incarnation."[25]

The relationship of the faith to cultures has been experienced since the very beginnings of the Church. Present-day thinking enables us to better understand the nature of Jesus' relationship with the culture of his milieu, as well as the relations of the early Christian community with the Jewish community and with all Gentile cultures. The process has continued through history, implanting the Church in all nations.

## BUILD THE CHURCH ACCORDING TO ITS IDENTITY

A second criterion of inculturation is fidelity to the essential identity of Christianity as lived in the Church. The original teaching of the Church, its theological and moral doctrine, its pastoral and legal practice, and its liturgy have been enriched and deepened by generations of believers, pastors, thinkers, and saints. Their contributions are an integral part of the Christian heritage. It would be impossible to dissociate living Christianity from all the enrichment it has received from councils, the Fathers of the Church, and great theologians. They all have helped to bring the body of the Church to maturity. The Church would not be what it is without an Augustine, an Origen, an

Athanasius, a Cyril, a Methodius, a Thomas Aquinas, a Francis of Assisi, a Teresa of Avila, or a Francis Xavier.

Of course, the Church of the past expressed itself in specific languages and in thought categories bound up with specific cultures, but recognition of such cultural interdependence does not nullify the perduring value and basic meaning of dogmatic formulations and ways of conceptualizing the faith, of basic sacramental and liturgical structures. Over the centuries, the advances in theological reflection, biblical exegesis, the history of dogma, spiritual doctrines, conciliar and canonical formulations are due to a maturation of faith as it was lived in both the Eastern and Western Churches, parts of the universal Church. The Church of the future will continue to grow out of the same roots and the same common stem that link it historically to its beginnings.

Thus, one of the primary laws of inculturation is to announce Christ to all cultures so that the Church may grow in them in accordance with its own proper nature and its own perduring identity. Inculturation, in other words, permits the Church to grow historically in accordance with the laws of its own proper growth. This is a point that must be clearly understood. The fundamental identity of the Church refers both to its *unity* and its *catholicity*. The Church's identity is not that of a uniform, undifferentiated system but rather that of a living body, which is an organism composed of vital parts, all contributing to the enrichment and unity of the entire body.

Vatican II clearly reaffirmed this organic conception of Church oneness. Indeed, the role of the Chair of Peter is precisely that of presiding over the "universal communion of charity," protecting all legitimate forms of variety in the Church and, at the same time, making sure that "particular elements serve unity rather than harm it." [26]

In his talk to the Roman Curia on December 22, 1984, John Paul commented on this central passage of *Lumen Gentium*. He wished to show how the universal Church derives enrichment from the life of all the particular Churches and, also indirectly, from all cultures, all nations, all languages, and all the achievements of human civilizations. Said John Paul II:

It would be difficult to express it more clearly or profoundly. The universal Church is presented as a communion of Churches (of particular churches) and, indirectly, as a community of nations, languages, and cultures. Each of them contributes its own "gifts" to the whole, as do every generation, every epoch, every scientific and social achievement, and every newly reached level of civilization.[27]

Thus, the identity of the Church presupposes a communion among all the particular Churches deriving their life from the "identical mystery of Christ." Each particular Church living in a specific culture must harmonize its experience with the experiences of all Churches. Otherwise, those experiences will not truly be "experiences of the Church," as John Paul II puts it.

Here we have the guiding principle for any and all inculturation that seeks to promote the growth of one and the same Church within diverse cultures. Identicalness is not opposed to particularities; it reveals its authenticity in the building up of communion and in the growth of the universal body of the Church. That brings us to our third criterion of inculturation: pluralism within the one Church.

## Reconcile Unity and Pluralism

A third criterion for inculturation has to do with the relationship between pluralism and unity in the Church. Safeguarding the identity of Christianity is in no way opposed to a healthy pluralism. Such pluralism has found expression in the particular Churches since the very beginning. Long ago, the history of the Eastern Churches anticipated and embodied the pluralism that is now manifested in the concrete life of the Churches and the plurality of human cultures. Commemorating the fourth centenary of the Pontifical Greek College in Rome in 1977, Paul VI recalled that fact:

It is precisely in the Eastern Churches that we find anticipated and perfectly demonstrated the validity of the pluralistic scheme. Thus modern researchers, seeking to verify

the relationships between Gospel proclamation and
human civilizations, between faith and culture, find in the
history of those venerable Churches significant early elab-
orations of concepts and concrete forms directed to the
binomial, unity and diversity (15).

Paul VI went on to say that the Church "welcomes that sort of
pluralism as an articulation of unity itself."[28]

Having clearly affirmed the adherence of ecclesial communities to this one communion in the faith, the Church unhesi-
tatingly accepts a pluralism made up of discernment, fidelity,
and ongoing investigation in the Gospel encounter with the
diversity of cultures. Speaking to the bishops of Africa and Madagascar, Paul VI affirmed that there must be fidelity to "the
essential, identical heritage, the selfsame doctrine of Christ, that
is professed by the authentic, authoritative tradition of the one,
true Church." But in the name of that very same fidelity, we
must be wise enough to discover new ways and expressions of
evangelization. This, he added, calls for "deeper investigation
of the cultural traditions of different populations, and of their
underlying philosophical notions, in order to pinpoint those elements that are not in contradiction with the Christian religion
or that can contribute to the enrichment of theological reflection."[29]

Unity is not uniformity. Paul VI expressed the Church's position in nuanced terms: "If the Church is to be Catholic first and
foremost, a pluralism of expression in the unity of substance is
legitimate and even desirable when it comes to professing a
common faith in one and the same Jesus Christ."[30] The ultimate
norm remains the *communio Ecclesiae*, Church communion, and
it holds true for all efforts to inculturate, adapt, or indigenize
theology, Church discipline, and pastoral work. The rule laid
down by Paul VI in the talk cited above is summed up in his
phrase, "a pluralism of expression in the unity of substance."

In short, true pluralism is that which creates *communion*. On
this point John Paul II reminded the Roman Curia of the teaching of Vatican II, and specifically of its thinking in *Lumen Gentium* (No. 13). There the Council noted that the universal
Church is a communion of particular Churches. Comments John

Paul II: "This document brings out the possibilities inherent in a healthy pluralism, but it also spells out very clearly its limits. True pluralism is never a divisive factor; it is something that helps to build unity in the universal communion of the Church."[31]

Inculturation requires the respect of differences but also the integration of diversities in a living communion. This is a basic theological criterion for inculturation, as it was clearly formulated by the Extraordinary Synod of Bishops of 1985:

> From this perspective we also find the theological principle for the problems of inculturation. Because the Church is communion, which joins diversity and unity in being present throughout the world, it takes from every culture all that it encounters of positive value. Yet inculturation is different from a simple external adaptation, because it means the intimate transformation of authentic cultural values through their integration of Christianity in the various human cultures.[32]

## PROMOTE DISCERNMENT AND INVESTIGATION

The fourth criterion of inculturation has to do with *discernment*, understood in the broadest sense and therefore including practical judgment and methodological reflection. For one thing, there must be deeper theological and anthropological investigation, if we are to confidently promote mutual encounter between the faith and living cultures. As Vatican II pointed out, the particular Churches are also rooted in Christ and built up on the foundation of the Apostles and universal tradition. They must submit the teaching of the Church to "fresh scrutiny" and deeper exploration in order to discover, in the surrounding cultures, the elements that can be integrated into Christian living, Church discipline, and the liturgy, as well as to see how faith can illuminate and enrich the native genius of each and every people. Vatican II suggests that, in each major socio-cultural area, theological reflection and investigation of this sort should be undertaken so that the young Churches may "take to themselves in a wonderful exchange all the riches of the nations that were given to Christ as an inheritance."[33]

This presupposes an ability to understand cultures, their potential receptivity to the Gospel message, and their possible contribution to the life of the Church. Attentive discernment is required. Insofar as indigenous cultures do not contradict Gospel values, they should be welcomed with respect and preserved. Christians should reverently and gladly lay bare "the seeds of the Word that lie hidden in them."[34] What elements should be considered in this process of discernment? Vatican II says that we should focus respectful attention on a people's customs, traditions, sciences, arts, disciplines, view of life and the social order, and religious traditions. In areas that do not affect the faith or the welfare of the whole community, the Church does not require a rigid uniformity. This holds true for the liturgy, as well:

> Even in the liturgy, the Church has no wish to impose a rigid uniformity in matters which do not involve the faith or the good of the whole community. Rather, the Church respects and fosters the spiritual adornments and gifts of the various races and peoples. Anything in their way of life that is not indissolubly bound up with superstition and error is studied with sympathy and, if possible, preserved intact. Sometimes, in fact, the Church admits such things into the liturgy itself, as long as they harmonize with its true and authentic spirit.[35]

An attitude of respect and esteem for non-Christian religions will prove to be a fruitful means of inculturation. They are "living expressions of the soul of vast human groups" and echo "thousands of years of the search for God." They often posses "an impressive heritage of profoundly religious texts." They are sprinkled with countless "seeds of the Word" and can be an authentic "preparation for the Gospel," to use the fine phrase that Vatican II borrowed from Eusebius of Caesarea.[36]

If we base our efforts of inculturation on solid theological discernment, we need not fear reductionism or confusion. Our efforts at inculturation will continue to enrich not only the local Churches but also the universal Church:

> Thus, every appearance of syncretism and of false particularism can be excluded, and Christian life can be accommodated to the genius and dispositions of each culture. Particular traditions, together with the individual heritage of each family of nations, can be illumined by the light of the gospel message and then taken up into Catholic unity.[37]

The particular Churches are historically identified "with the persons, but also with the riches and limitations, the ways of praying, loving, and viewing life and the world, that mark a given human ensemble." For them, the task of inculturation is "to assimilate the essential core of the gospel message, transpose it, without any betrayal of its essential truth, into the language those human beings understand, and then proclaim it in that language."[38]

Inculturation essentially presupposes an attitude of receptivity and discernment. This is a complicated and difficult task. As Vatican II indicated, it calls for a serious effort of investigation in each of the major socio-cultural areas of the world. Africa is much concerned by that kind of reflection and research.[39]

## THE AFRICAN EXPERIENCE OF INCULTURATION

Observing the experience of the Church in its effort to evangelize specific cultures helps us understand more concretely the meaning of inculturation. In this chapter we will concentrate our attention on the historical experience of inculturation in Africa. In no other continent have the recent Popes been so explicit and forceful as to the necessity and conditions of inculturation today. Their teaching imparts values not only limited to Africa; it concerns all nations where the Gospel of Christ is to be announced. The visits of Paul VI and John Paul II to Africa have stimulated a new approach to the evangelization of African cultures and paved the way to a renewed understanding of inculturation.[40]

## AN AFRICAN EXPRESSION OF CATHOLIC IDENTITY

Paul VI was a true pioneer in boldly and lucidly broaching the problems of evangelization in modern Africa.

As far back as 1969, when Paul VI was in Uganda, he spoke to the assembled bishops of Africa and laid down solid guidelines for the work of inculturation on this continent. He told the Africans that henceforth they were to be their own missionaries, and he asked how the Church was to grow in Africa. He focused on two points that clearly and firmly embody the guiding principles for all inculturation: *fidelity to the essential heritage* deriving from the Church of Christ and an *African expression* of that heritage, so that a truly African Christianity could develop.

First, said Paul VI, your Church must be Catholic above all else, that is, "wholly grounded on one and the same identical, essential heritage, the teaching of Christ, that is professed by the authentic, authorized tradition of the one true Church." That means fidelity to the doctrine and deposit of faith that belong to the Church of all times, because we ourselves do not invent faith in Christ and we cannot let other forms of religiousness supplant our adherence to the Church of Jesus Christ.

This first point calls for a second. Christianity must penetrate deeply into the native genius and culture of Africa, as a legitimate pluralism requires. Africans can and should have a Christianity that is African in its expression. This is the second principle of inculturation invoked by Paul VI: "The expression, that is the language, the way of manifesting the one and only faith, can be manifold and therefore original, in line with the language, style, temperament, genius, and culture of those professing this one faith. In this respect a pluralism is legitimate and even desirable." Paul VI mentions the domains where inculturation is needed: the pastoral, ritual, educational and spiritual domains. Thus, African culture can be the primary beneficiary of the riches that Christianity brings to all peoples and civilizations.

Pluralism is legitimate and desirable, said Paul VI, but there can be no healthy pluralism without attentive discernment. He did not hesitate to point out the dangers that may crop up, particularly when it is a matter of "religious pluralism." We must make sure that profession of the Christian faith does not become "a form of local folklore, exclusivist racism, egotistical tribalism, or arbitrary separatism." Grounded on a solid faith, Africans will not only avoid these pitfalls but also ensure that their growth as Christians brings enrichment to the universal Church. "You will be able to formulate Catholicism in terms that are completely suited to your culture and to offer the Catholic Church the precious and original contribution of 'negritude,' of which it has particular need at this point in history."[41]

## MISSIONARY IMPULSE ALWAYS NECESSARY

The broad lines of what Paul VI said in Uganda can be found in his Message to Africa in 1967, *Africae Terrarum*. In this important message he also elaborated a retrospective view of the work of missionaries in Africa. While acknowledging their limitations, he also underlined their undeniable merits in the work of evangelization. Paul VI readily admitted that missionaries may have failed to comprehend African ways and ancient traditions. They could not completely escape the mentality of their age, and they did not always manage to achieve an in-depth understanding of the customs and history of the people they were evangelizing. But the universal Church and the African Church must recognize and appreciate "their heroic undertaking." Their sole desire was to bring the Gospel message to Africans: "Out of love for Christ, the missionaries left their family and homeland, and a large number of them sacrificed their lives for the good of Africa."

Paul VI reminds us that very often missionaries were pioneers, bringing "the first forms of school education and health assistance, the first friendly contact with the rest of humanity, the first introduction to and exploration of knowledge data that are taken for granted today as elements of worldwide culture." Some missionaries pursued worthy anthropological studies. The inculturation of the Gospel message will now proceed by way of internal growth or indigenization, but that does not mean the end of all missionary aid from other Churches.[42]

Inculturation rightly lays stress on the indigenization of local Churches because Christians intimately familiar with a national culture will be the best evangelizers of their milieu. But indigenization cannot be set in opposition to missionary work. Native bishops are the first to condemn any hint of rejecting missionary cooperation. The bishops of Africa and Madagascar, for example, had this to say:

> We denounce as contrary to the Gospel message and the Church's authentic teaching any and every act and spoken or written word that might hinder cooperation between the young Churches and the ancient Churches. This clear-cut stand on our part should suffice to rekindle the missionary impulse in generous souls who believe it is still possible today to serve the Church at home and abroad.[43]

Having said that, the bishops also point out that missionary activity should assume new forms in the future, forms that show respect for the legitimate autonomy of local Churches and their own proper responsibility.

We must also acknowledge the missionary work done by other Christian denominations. In fact, they are in friendly competition with Catholic missionaries, insofar as they participate in the work of evangelization. Paul VI recognized the merits of both Catholic and non-Catholic missionaries. When he canonized the martyrs of Uganda, in 1964, he said: "It was the White Fathers who introduced Catholicism into Uganda, preaching the Gospel message in friendly competition with Anglican missionaries. As their reward for facing incalculable dangers and labors, they had the good fortune to be the educators in Christ of the martyrs whom we celebrate today as heroic brothers in the faith and patrons in the glory of heaven."[44]

The spirit of ecumenism should continue to motivate all Christians engaged in the task of inculturating the Gospel in Africa.[45]

## CHURCH GROWING WITH AFRICAN CULTURE

Today the bishops and Christians of Africa are the ones continuing and extending the first efforts at evangelization. Speaking more specifically to African intellectuals, Paul VI said:

Africa needs you, your study, your research, your art, your teaching, not only for its past to be appreciated but also for its new culture to ripen on the ancient trunk and grow strong in the fruitful quest for truth. Faced with the technical and industrial growth that has reached your Continent, your specific task is to ensure the vitality of the values of the human mind and spirit.[46]

The visible results of evangelization are the proof that Christianity has been solidly implanted in cultures. Addressing a symposium of the Episcopal Conferences of Africa and Madagascar in 1975, Paul VI took joy in the fact that Christianity had progressed so rapidly. A few decades had produced amazing results: a native episcopate, many vocations, vital communities, admirable catechists, and even the witness of humble Christians as martyrs. "Is not all that the mark of an authentic Christianity?"[47]

Inculturation does not mean a merely external adaptation of Christianity to a culture. It is from within that the Gospel message must enrich civilizations. Meeting the bishops of Africa on October 29, 1977, the tenth anniversary of his message *Africae Terrarum*, Paul VI spelled out this organic law: "The authentically Christian, Catholic faith has been grafted, as it were, on the venerable ancestral trunk; it is that faith that should give quality and savor to the fruits of the tree."[48]

Among the fruits to be expected from the Church's work in Africa is the transformation of societies in justice and peace. Through their sincere and generous commitment, Catholics make clear the renewing power of the Gospel message and bear witness to the Church's contribution to the unselfish service in African societies. Paul VI urges Africans to discover the Church's contributions to the cultures of Africa: "Don't be afraid of the church. It honors you. It educates upright, loyal citizens for you. It does not foment rivalries or divisions. It seeks to promote healthy liberty, social justice, and peace. If it has any preference, it is for the education of children and the common people, for the needs of those who are suffering or abandoned."[49]

## Fully Christians and Fully Africans

John Paul II has clearly reaffirmed the message of his predecessor, and he further explicited the tasks of inculturation in Africa. The aim is to Africanize the Church so that the Gospel may penetrate all areas of private and social life. In his visits to Africa, he has explained over and over again how to understand the concrete tasks of inculturation and Africanization that are indispensable for a successful evangelization of the continent. Addressing the bishops of Zaire and many other African bishops gathered in Kinshasa in 1980, he declared: "One of the aspects of this evangelization is the inculturation of the Gospel message, the Africanization of the Church. Several people have told me that it is a matter very close to your hearts, and rightly so. It is a part of the indispensable efforts to incarnate the message of Christ."[50] Very concretely, the Pope mentions some of the vital areas that deserve to be explored with a view to effective inculturation of the Gospel message: the language that the Christian message should assume, catechesis, theological reflection, suitably adapted expressions of the liturgy and sacred art, and the communitarian forms of Christian life.

Africans, he said, must be able to integrate elements deriving from different sources. Those sources would include the biblical culture, the historical cultures in which Christianity has matured over the centuries, and the new cultures to which the Gospel message is addressed:

> In my apostolic exhortation on catechetics [*Catechesi Tradendae 1979*, No. 53], I myself called attention to the fact that the Gospel message cannot be detached purely and simply from the biblical culture in which it was first inserted, nor even, without serious losses, from the cultures in which it found expression over the centuries; and that, in addition, the power of the Gospel message is transforming and regenerative everywhere.

In the area of catechetics, John Paul II indicates that presentations should be adapted more to the African soul, while taking into account cultural interchanges with the rest of the world. In the area of liturgy he says, "A whole enrichment is possible, provided that the meaning of the Christian rite is well preserved at all times and that the universal, Catholic aspect of the Church (the 'substantial unity of the Roman Rite') shows up clearly, in union with the other local Churches and in accord with the Holy See." In the area of ethics, a welcome must be extended to all the resources of the African soul that are so many stepping stones to Christianity. Africans must be able to discern them: "You know them better than anyone, those that have to do with the spiritual view of life, the sense of family, children, community life, and the like. As is true in every civilization, there are other features that are less favorable."[51] On his third trip to Africa, in August 1985, John Paul was even more explicit in encouraging "a tireless effort at inculturation."[52] He uses new and suggestive formulations to describe it. Inculturation is the "concrete form of the covenant between God and human beings in this time and place." Or, "It is the welcome acceptance of the universal truth by a human community endowed with its own specific sensibility and shaped by its own long quest for the meaning of life."[53]

John Paul II does not hesitate to specify again the concrete areas where evangelization should bear its fruits: "daily life . . . mentalities . . . institutions." He spells this out in detail: the animation of rural and urban life, the improvement of crop yield, cooperation, literacy training, work among artisans, domestic training, the promotion of women, health education, housing, and the defense of rights.[54] Lay people have a special responsibility to bring the spirit of the Gospel into all areas of the temporal order. During his visit in Nigeria, the Pope urged them "to bring the spirit of Christ into such spheres of life as marriage and the family, trade and commerce, the arts and professions, politics and government, culture and national and international relations. In all these areas lay people must, in the expression of the Second Vatican Council, play their own distinctive role."[55]

The work of inculturation should take due account of the millennial experiences of traditional religions and customs. Prudent discernment is needed to retain what is sound and compatible with the Christian ideal, but also to break when necessary with what is opposed to God's revelation or with what might be tainted with syncretistic practices and superstition.

Religious dialogue is linked with the work of inculturation because religious traditions are the expression of rich cultural traditions. But dialogue, necessary as it is, should not prevent the Church from proclaiming the Gospel. Speaking to the Nigerian bishops in Rome in 1987, the Pope said:

> In a multireligious society such as Nigeria, where there are an almost equal number of Muslims and Christians and many adherents of traditional African religions, I encourage you to reaffirm the commitment of the Catholic Church to both dialogue and to the proclamation of the Gospel. There can be no question of choosing one and ignoring or rejecting the other.[56]

Moreover, Africans of all creeds and convictions are trying to incorporate the achievements of modern civilizations. They are to do it with a moral freedom permitting them to avoid the materialistic mentality that often accompanies technological culture.[57]

The bolder inculturation seeks to be, the more it will presuppose serious searching and a sound spiritual formation. John Paul II reminds the bishops of Cameroon of this fact: "Hence the place that you will rightly give to the inculturation of the Gospel message and dialogue between religions. As I explained to your intellectuals this afternoon, this presupposes a profoundly Christian and even theological formation to achieve fruitful results without losing Catholic identity."[58] Fortunately, that search is moving forward in Africa, both in the Church and in society. In that the pope sees a sign of hope for the mutual enrichment of cultures: "We must welcome as an opportunity the fact that we are seeing ongoing interchanges among intellectuals, scholars, social workers, economists, and spiritual authorities."[59]

The message of Paul VI and John Paul II is full of daring and discernment. The Church is making the cultural yearnings of the African continent its own. John Paul II acknowledges it in a phrase that reveals the full scope of the inculturation to be achieved. He urges Africans to be simultaneously "fully Christians and fully Africans."[60]

To achieve the fullness of inculturation, the Gospel will have to permeate progressively all legitimate expectations of African culture. One of the greatest aspirations of African men and women is to preserve the lasting value of their rich traditions, while striving for the human advantage of modernization. The cultural challenge of Africans is to reconcile the values of historical wisdom with modern progress, and yet maintain alive their proper identity. The task of evangelization should consider both these dimensions — traditional and modern — of living cultures.

Referring to the past heritage of Africa, John Paul II summed up the task of inculturation, which calls for the full respect of cultures and the integral proclamation of the Gospel:

> By respecting, preserving and fostering the particular values and riches of your people's cultural heritage, you will be in a position to lead them to a better understanding of the mystery of Christ, which is to be lived in the noble, concrete and daily experiences of African life. There is no question of adulterating the word of God, or of emptying the cross of its power (cf. 1 Cor. 1:17), but rather of bringing Christ into the very center of African life and of lifting up all African life to Christ. Thus not only is Christianity relevant to Africa, but Christ, in the members of his Body, is himself African.[61]

Inculturation's goal is finally *to make Christ become African* in the members of his Body.

## FUTURE DEVELOPMENT AND MODERN CULTURE

Looking toward the future, the Catholics of Africa will share the responsibility of the universal Church in regard to the construction of a just and peaceful world. The task of development is not only a technological problem. It is basically an ethical, cultural and spiritual concern; it pursues the integral progress of each person and all peoples. It confronts all levels of poverty—economic, social cultural, spiritual. The Church has a special compassion for the poorest among the poor, for those "who live without hope," as John Paul II calls them in *Sollicitudo Rei Socialis*. We understand better today that development is linked with the proclamation of the Gospel.

Modern development is a movement in the history of Creation, obscured by human sins, in need of Redemption.[62] "The concept of faith makes quite clear the reasons which impel the Church to concern herself with the problems of development, to consider them a duty of her pastoral ministry, and to urge all to think about the nature and characteristics of authentic human development."[63]

Development in Africa, as everywhere, will not come without deep cultural changes. What direction will that cultural transformation take? Will it be passively experienced or intentionally oriented? How can it be inspired by Christian values? Those are the decisive questions for the future of the Church. How should it face the new culture that accompanies modernization? Confronting the culture of modernity will be one of the greatest challenges of Africans engaged in the task of inculturation.[64] Modernity is a way of life linked with industrialization and urbanization. Modern mentality represents a *new culture* penetrating all countries and all social groups. In Africa, modern lifestyles and values are spreading fast through the cities and the media, through new conception of family life, production, consumption, work, leisure, information, education.

Modernity has brought to humanity immense advantages in all sectors of life: health, education, industry, agriculture, communication, transport, government, administration. All peoples around the world aspire to share these advantages. But when this new culture spreads in the world, it challenges the traditional institutions and values which had, over centuries, structured human societies and given them stability. Affected most is the institution of the family, with grave consequences for personal, social, and religious life. Other key sectors undergo radical changes: modes of education, styles of work, relationships with nature, religious customs, rites, and celebrations—all aspects of life closely linked with traditional religion.

Studying these cultural changes and their spiritual significance for the person, the family, the society, and the Church will require competent and concerted efforts on the part of all Catholics. The task exceeds the capacity of a single bishop, pastor, or lay person. A collective effort is needed. One is urgently reminded of the recommendation of Vatican II that each sociocultural region undertake a special study in order to understand better how faith can answer the needs of living cultures.[65]

## LEARNING INCULTURATION THROUGH LIFE

On several occasions, John Paul II has acknowledged the results that have been achieved through the practice of inculturation in Africa. Yet a better understanding of the process is still needed. This will require a renewed theological reflection on the mysterious reciprocity of Christ's Incarnation with all human cultures. On his sixth apostolic visit, John Paul II noted, in Chad, the efforts that have been made toward inculturation in different spheres, particularly with the liturgy, translations, chants, and adapted catechesis. When he spoke to the bishops, he presented a developed, integrated view of this process, saying that proclamation of the Gospel leads to a transformation of the authentic values of the various cultures, so that they can be integrated into Christianity.

> The founding event of Pentecost reminds us in an exemplary manner that all the peoples of the earth are called to proclaim the "wonders of God" in the plurality and diversity of their languages. Inculturation . . . is thus inherent in proclamation of the Gospel. . . . A carefully structured, rigorous theological reflection is needed in order to appreciate the customs, traditions, wisdom, knowledge, arts and disciplines of different people, so that all that is true, good and beautiful in their heritage can enter into "the wonderful reciprocity" of Christ's Incarnation.[66]

## INCULTURATION: A CENTRAL THEME OF THE AFRICAN SYNOD

Keeping in mind the main points of the preceding discussion, it appears quite natural that the question of inculturation should now be considered one of the central themes of the African Synod. The members of the Council of the Secretary General of the Special Assembly for the Synod of the Bishops of Africa met in Rome in 1989. The Pope received them on June 24, tracing the main lines of orientation for the coming assembly: "The joint reflection should cover all the important aspects of the life of the Church in Africa, and in particular should include *evangelization, inculturation, dialogue, pastoral care in social areas*, and the *means of social communication.*" With regard to inculturation, the Holy Father declared:

> Just as Jesus in proclaiming the Gospel used all the elements which made up the culture of his people, so the Church too must use elements taken from human cultures in order to build the Kingdom. However, *inculturation* does not mean just an external adaptation. Inculturation means the intimate transformation of authentic cultural values through the integration of Christianity in the various human cultures.

## SUMMING UP: INCULTURATION IS ESSENTIAL TO THE CHURCH'S MISSION

The Church's long experience in inculturating the Gospel has greatly enriched the theology of evangelization and has led to a renewed formulation of Catholic thought concerning inculturation.

The teaching of the Church on inculturation has now been clearly formulated and incorporated in the new encyclical on the missions, *Redemptoris Missio* (1990). In its fifth chapter, it illustrates the "paths of mission" and the place of inculturation in the missionary project of the Church: the initial proclamation of Christ the Savior, conversion and baptism, forming local churches, ecclesial basic communities, inculturation, interreligious dialogue, and development. "Inculturation means the intimate transformation of authentic cultural values through their integration in Christianity and the insertion of Christianity in the various human cultures. The process is thus a profound and all-embracing one, which involves the Christian message and also the Church's reflection and practice." Inculturation makes the Church a more intelligible sign and a more effective instrument of mission. Through the inculturation of the local churches, "the universal Church herself is enriched with forms of expression and values in the various sectors of Christian life, such as evangelization, worship, theology and charitable works. She comes to know and express better the mystery of Christ, all the while being motivated to continual renewal." Such inculturation requires patient discernment, guided by two principles: "compatibility with the gospel and communion with the universal Church. Inculturation, as all of life, takes time. As Pope Paul VI said in Kampala in 1969: 'It will require an incubation of the Christian mystery in the genius of your people in order that its native voice more clearly and frankly may then be raised harmoniously in the chorus of other voices in the universal Church.' " Inculturation is the expression of the life within the community and not exclusively the result of erudite research. "The safeguarding of traditional values is the work of a mature faith."[67]

In the light of the Church's experience and formal teaching, we understand better today the urgent necessity and yet the complex requirements of inculturating the Gospel in all cultural milieus. It is an inherent necessity of evangelization and a concrete aspect of the Incarnation. Those committed to evangelization are more aware nowadays of what it means to convert, elevate, and redeem human cultures. Converting the personal conscience and converting the collective conscience are very closely linked. Such a challenge calls for a continued effort of pastors, practitioners, and researchers in the whole Church.

In conclusion, then, we see that the renewed interest of the Church in inculturation is the sign of a more conscious and concerted effort to evangelize all cultures. Inculturation and evangelization are inseparable: the Church pursues the inculturation of the Gospel in order to evangelize cultures. John Paul II insists equally on both tasks, indicating the conditions of their implementation:

> You are aware that inculturation commits the Church to a path that is difficult, but necessary. Pastors, theologians

and the specialists in the human sciences must also collaborate closely, so that this vital process may come about in a way that benefits both the evangelized and the evangelizers, in order to avoid any simplification or undue haste that would end in syncretism or a secular reduction of the proclamation of the Gospel. Carry out your research on these questions serenely and in depth, aware that your work will help many in the Church—and not only in what are called "mission lands."[68]

This evangelical project calls for a renewal and mobilization of the whole Church.

# 4

# Can We Still Hear a
# Counter-Cultural Prophet?

The difficult task of inculturating the Gospel in modern society requires us to become cultural critics and to discern in our
own culture traits that are dehumanizing. It is not always easy
to be critical of one's culture, since we so naturally and unconsciously identify with our own cultural milieu. At times we need
the voice of prophets to stir us and to expose the threatening
effects of anti-culture in our society. Secular writers, thinkers,
and novelists can have a lot to say to us about anti-cultural
trends in the modern world. One such writer was George Orwell,
a forceful and passionate prophet of dehumanization within
modern society. Let us briefly recall his extraordinary experience
and message.

In 1948, Eric Blair, already gravely ill, was completing his
final novel, *The Last Man in Europe,* which appeared ultimately
under a pseudonym, with another title suggested by the pub-
lisher. The book was *1984,* the author, George Orwell.

The changes in the author's name and in the title of the book
give us an insight into understanding his hidden significance for
our own culture.

## NEGATIVE UTOPIA

Rereading this novel, written at the end of an exceptional
literary career, more than forty years after its appearance, leads

us to apply Orwell's message to our own culture, which is no less menaced and anguished than the world of 1948. Yet our culture, which appears to embody immense aspirations and universal expectations, leaves room for a great deal of hope.

The original title, *The Last Man in Europe,* merits particular attention and suggests reading *1984* as a parable of premonition about the fatal destiny of humankind. To whom is this parable addressed, to what ideal reader? To us all, to all men and women of our time. Let us read it then as *an allegory of anti-culture* that concerns all human beings.

Before proceeding with this explication, which one could call cultural and moral, we must acknowledge that the novel *1984,* perhaps more than some other works of fiction, is open to innumerable interpretations.

There have been many keys to the reading of *1984*: literary, historical, political, philosophical, ethical, or psychoanalytical. Orwell himself was disheartened by the arguments among literary critics. How could his novel be seen, at one and the same time, as an indictment of degenerate capitalism, an anticommunist lampoon, a diatribe against the Labour Party, an unconscious revolt against a form of education, or even an attack on the BBC in London, where Orwell worked for several years in Office 101 – the number of the notorious Room 101 in the Ministry of Love in his novel. Other critics, in scrutinizing the novel as a brilliant exercise in prophecy, counted 132 predictions made by Orwell in 1948, 120 of which were alleged to have come true by 1984.

*The Last Man in Europe,* Orwell's original title, strikes me primarily as a negative Utopia written by an indignant observer who, before dying, utters a cry of despair in order to rouse all humankind, all his brothers and sisters, dramatically imploring them to save themselves, if possible, from collective suicide. This parody of despair is just as deeply distressing in our day, for the dehumanization of our societies has progressed relentlessly. That undoubtedly explains why a novel written in 1948 still raises questions in our minds and disquiets us, as only an inspired piece of writing can do.

If we interpret *1984* as the parable of anti-beatitude, we discern in it a tale denouncing the desecration of humankind, and at the same time a lucid provocation, calling, in spite of everything, for a new surge of hope. Read in this way, *1984* is not a mere clinical report of a political disaster, but rather a vehement appeal for the moral liberation of every person on earth.

Eric Blair appears to have been a man wounded by life — by his errors, moral humiliations, and admitted disgrace, yet in him was a flame that could never be extinguished. One surmises that Orwell was a convinced European, nostalgic and intractable before the sacrilegious attacks against the humanist ideal that continued to consume him, in spite of all adversity.

## BIG BROTHER IS WATCHING YOU

Seen from this angle, *1984* reads as a horrifying satire which describes "the last man," enslaved by totalitarian regimes geared toward a permanent obsession with war. We come to ask ourselves why the author is so relentless in his condemnation of Big Brother and why he dwells with disturbing verisimilitude on the torments this inhuman brute inflicts on his victim, Winston Smith. For, after all, what has the poor man done? Winston Smith is an ordinary man, condemned precisely because he had the mad idea of behaving as people ought to behave in everyday life. He committed the irreparable crime: he had the temerity to act as a free citizen, picturing himself foiling the supervision of the powers that be and even rebelling against the perfection of the system. He had the criminal delusion that he could clandestinely seek a modicum of freedom. But Big Brother was watching.

His pathetic affair with Julia, in which they thought they could share a secret love safe from Big Brother's surveillance, was the cause of their downfall. The Party does everything to make the culprit see reason by means of inculcated Truth, rectified Thought, psychological rehabilitation, torture, and self-accusation. Winston Smith eventually understands the official meaning of life and supreme happiness. In his final delirium he imagines the bullet entering his brain, and at that point everything succeeds. Hate is transformed into love. "But it was all right, everything was all right, the struggle was finished. He had won the victory over himself. He loved Big Brother."

Why such a sarcastic rage against the enemies of this "last man," if not because George Orwell refuses to resign himself to the inevitable? He is haunted by an ideal image of humankind that he wants to defend, if necessary, with the weapons of literary violence, against the imminent, apparently inevitable but not yet accomplished catastrophe.

Orwell's conscience tells him that brother cannot kill brother, for that would be the end of humankind. But the excessive humiliation inflicted on Winston Smith makes him subhuman. Big Brother explains to his victim how the new being recreated by the system is the exact opposite of the human being that tradition has so far shaped: "already we are breaking down the habits of thought which have survived from before the Revolution. . . . If you want a picture of the future, imagine a boot stamping on a human face—forever." This is the antithesis of the human model bequeathed to us by a Greco-Roman culture and Jewish and Christian traditions: a responsible being capable of love and reason, creator of history and culture, artisan of progress, master of a collective destiny, open to transcendence, and turned toward hope.

## ANTI-BIBLICAL PARODIES

What does Winston Smith represent to us? Is he not the symbol, albeit inverted and untenable, of traditional humanism, which imparts to human beings their full value and dignity? Is it not for the sake of this ideal that Orwell wages his battle with a religious fervor reminiscent of the wrath of the Old Testament prophets?

It is no misconception to credit the author with genuine spiritual and moral compassion for human beings as such. Several commentators have linked Orwell's name with those of the great English moralists, comparing him with Swift or Hobbes. At the end of his life, Orwell confided that the impetus for his writing had always come from an injustice to be remedied or a falsehood to be uncovered.

Let us not forget that George Orwell was British, educated in the classic humanist tradition, and not lacking in religious formation. He attended St. Cyprian's Preparatory School and then studied at Eton. We know as well that he requested a religious burial and was interred at All Saints Cemetery. At first, some were surprised by this, but as his biographer Bernard Crick points out, there was nothing surprising in it: "he loved the earth, his country, and the liturgical language of the Anglican Church."

I believe it was Orwell's moral and spiritual attitude that gave him the almost prophetic strength to condemn Big Brother's perversion of the most sacred values of the Jewish and Christian traditions. Look at the anti-biblical parodies he invents with disconcerting genius. The anti-biblical counterfeit is perfect: it destroys such sacred realities as the God of love, fraternity, truth, peace, freedom of conscience, and venerated traditions. Everything is exactly the opposite for Big Brother in *1984*. God can be nothing other than brutal power: "God is Power." Big Brother represents the antithesis of fraternity, the monster who murders his brother. "Freedom is Slavery." Love is nothing but the pursuit of destructive hatred under the control of the notorious Ministry of Love. The hallmark of the Ministry of Truth is the opposite of truth. History—that is, human memory—is completely abolished and rewritten. Peace is a state of permanent war: "by becoming continuous, war has ceased to exist. . . . War is Peace."

Humans are no longer created in God's image. As Big Brother triumphantly says, "we create human nature." Speech itself, the supreme human attribute, is desecrated by the counter-language of Newspeak, in which such words as *honor, justice, morality,* and *religion* have been completely abolished.

Winston Smith eventually appears before Big Brother like the damned at the last judgment. "Winston," O'Brien says, "you are the last man. Your kind is extinct. . . . You are outside history, you are non-existent." This is hell; this is being cast into the outer darkness.

If God is obliterated from people's memories, who can oppose Big Brother? O'Brien asks Winston,

"Do you believe in God, Winston?"

"No."

"Then what is it, this principle that will defeat us?"

The reversal of the biblical conception of humankind is complete, as is brutally apparent from O'Brien's satanic proclamation: "the old civilizations claimed that they were founded on love or justice. Ours is founded upon hatred. In our world there will be no emotions except fear, rage, triumph, and humiliation. Everything else we shall destroy—everything."

## DON'T LET IT HAPPEN

The drastic consequence of this desecration is the annihilation of human beings as represented by the values dearest to them. Big Brother gloats,

> we have cut the links between child and parent, and between man and man, and between man and woman. No one dares trust a wife or a child or a friend any longer. But in the future there will be no wives and no friends. Children will be taken from their mothers at birth, as one takes eggs from a hen. The sex instinct will be eradicated. Procreation will be an annual formality like the renewal of a ration card.

This paradigm of dehumanization prompted certain critics, including his friend, novelist Julian Symons, to attribute to Orwell the "quality of perversity" when it came to observation and polemics. Yet it can just as easily be interpreted as a reflection of religious anger concealing immense compassion for humankind—boundless concern which is not, however, devoid of hope.

Orwell chose a tone of execration as his means and wrote in parables, the better to fire people's imaginations and draw us back from the brink of the moral abyss held in store for us by societies geared up for war that must constantly be prepared for. "Stop before it is too late," he cried to his generation and to ours.

In reply to a journalist who, a few months before Orwell's death, asked him whether *1984* was a prediction for the Europe of the future, this prophet and moralist said:

> It is not exactly. After all, it is only a *parody*. I think something similar might happen, if the world were allowed to

continue in the direction it has taken. The Western countries are preparing for an all-out war with the Soviet Union, and this has necessitated a special social structure and a search of weapons, of which the atom bomb is merely the most conspicuous. But the danger also lies in the fact that intellectuals of all leanings accepted a totalitarian vision of the world. The moral is: "Don't let this happen."

George Orwell was a die hard; he would not bow to the law of brutal determinism that threatens to overtake our societies. In spite of the abomination he foresaw, he retained an absolute faith in the dignity and grandeur of humankind. There are several signs to convince us of this faith. After experiencing the appalling horrors of the Spanish Civil War, he said in *Homage to Catalonia*: "I have the worst memories of Spain but few unpleasant memories of Spaniards"; and he added a revealing phrase: "it is curious that nothing in my experience of Spain has undermined my faith in the dignity and goodness of human beings."

## CONDEMNED TO HOPE

In the final analysis, this parable of anti-humanism provides us with a salutary message that subsequent events have merely reinforced. Paradoxically, the tragedy of the world today condemns us to hope, for the future now depends solely on our moral courage — our collective genius. Admittedly, anti-culture and anti-humanism have, since 1948, been gaining ground with a virulence that Orwell had been unable to gauge. Atomic terror was to reach crisis level and is still threatening not only to destroy our bodies but also do damage to our minds. Ecological disasters may hold in store cataclysms that Orwell could hardly begin to imagine, any more than he could foresee the drastic energy crisis and soaring oil prices that triggered off a lingering conflict whose implications are more than just economic, as the Gulf War has shown. The degree to which the biological engineering of the future could go was hinted at in Big Brother's experiments. On an international plane, the wars of liberation from 1948 onward, the decline of the old colonial powers, the establishment of new geopolitical and military hegemonies, the rise of over a hundred new nations, the dramatic fragmentation of the Soviet Union and its empire in Europe, and the huge challenges of development are raising formidable problems of justice and even of pure survival for the world community. The use of satellites for communication — as well as for observation and combat — has redrawn the map of this small globe, bringing its inhabitants closer together for the purpose of both dialogue and confrontation. Ideological propaganda has become infinitely more scientific and seductively rivals sophisticated advertising. Microprocessors are doing wonders but are also providing the scientific branch of the police force with infallible instruments for scrutinizing our private lives, for we leave electronic traces behind us everywhere.

The impending threats to the future of human beings have not abated. They will continue to weigh on each of us and those who come after us. Humankind has no choice; from now on we must live with nuclear weapons, an endangered genetic heritage, and a threatened natural environment.

Since Orwell's time we have become collectively more aware of the dangers common to the entire human family. Perhaps we are now more aware that the challenge is within us. We cannot be freed solely by overthrowing political regimes or ideological systems. The worse disaster would be resignation — the death of hope. Losing faith in the capacity of human beings to build the society of the future would be the absolute catastrophe.

## CULTURE'S REVENGE

The premonitory messages of prophets such as Orwell and, in particular, the lesson of events since 1948, have helped us to revert to a key value — confidence in ourselves or, in other words, hope. Hope continues, in spite of everything, to uplift humankind. Facts have belied Orwell's fiction, but his underlying intentions have triumphed: there is no fatalism. Through the anguish oppressing all human beings today, hope springs eternal, as strong as life itself. Therein lies the true promise of a new start. Human beings feel so threatened that they are reverting to the essential, radical goal: to save the human race, for this is what is at stake. All is not lost, for there is always hope.

This is the revenge of culture—a transcending value to be defended. Collective anguish has had the surprising effect of making us introspective and causing us to look for salvation in ourselves. That is why culture, to quote John Paul II, has become "a vital sphere on which the destiny of the world at the end of the twentieth century depends" (*L'Osservatore Romano,* May 25, 1982).

Our generation still gives Orwell credit for having played the role of a "negative prophet," to borrow Paul Ricoeur's expression. He urges us to counter the parable of anti-culture with a humanist reply. By uncovering the untruths of totalitarianism, the traces of which are found in every society tempted to recognize the Supreme Being in the Party, the State, or the System, Orwell enables us to rediscover that humankind's true salvation lies in combating falsehood—in the enlightened conscience of each one of us. One must acknowledge, as Erich Fromm said, that Orwell does not prophesy disaster; he simply tries to stir us up. The impending threat is that of the perversion of language, which poisons and divides minds. It is intolerable that words such as *democracy, fraternity, love, peace, justice,* and *truth* should literally have become two-edged swords in the hands of enemy brothers. Orwell fought in defense of speech and truth, for, as he said, "the very concept of objective truth is dying out in the world." Over and above the infinite nostalgia which emanates from his novel, let us listen to his final message: Let us defend the truth of the human language, and hope will survive. Hope is a dynamic virtue that requires lucidity and courage.

By being cultural critics we are promoting the truth of language and of human dignity. At times we have to challenge and contest destructive contradictions in our culture. Celebrating the centenary of *Rerum Novarum,* John Paul II reminded us (Encyclical *Centesimus Annus,* May 1, 1991, No. 50) of the necessity of assessing critically the culture of our own nation: "From this open search for truth, which is renewed in every generation, the culture of a nation derives its character. Indeed, the heritage of values which has been received and handed down is always challenged by the young." The first test is one's own life and the recognition that the Gospel can redeem the culture of each nation. The alternative, adds John Paul II, could be cultural decadence: "when a culture becomes inward looking, and tries to perpetuate obsolete ways of living by rejecting any exchange or debate with regard to the truth about man, then it becomes sterile and is heading for decadence."

The crucial battle for human dignity is a moral, cultural, and educational one, for in the final analysis, everything depends on the ultimate meaning we give to our individual and collective destiny. It is culture that is at stake, for without culture there are no human beings. The culture of the future will definitely be a culture of hope.

# 5

# Toward a New Convergence of Science and Religion?

Up until a generation ago, it was commonly held among sociologists that when empirical sciences prevail in a given culture, religion is bound to decline and secularization sets in. Today that assumption is questioned by many sociologists and scientists themselves.

One observes that after a period dominated by positivism and empiricism, the scientific world is presently reexamining its ethical and spiritual attitudes. It is quite revealing to follow that evolution and its cultural significance.

## FROM ANIMISM TO EMPIRICISM?

If we look at the changing image of scientists and scholars over the centuries, we see that the intellectual masters of the past used to deal with the totality of knowledge available about the universe, the gods, the sacred, traditions, scriptures, the rules and codes of human behavior. This was the condition of the learned in Egypt, Mesopotamia, India, China, and Greece. Pythagoras himself said he was enraptured by the harmony of the universe and the "music of the spheres," and Aristotle wrote that "science was concerned with the necessary and the eternal."[1] This conviction remained firm until the time of Descartes, who maintained that "we can know nothing with certainty if we do not know first that God exists."[2]

But, as appears from the history of the sciences, this image of the scientist as one who studies both the Universe and its Creator, was all but destroyed by the advent of the Age of Reason. From now on, it was proclaimed, science would declare its total independence from religion, traditions, the holy scriptures, theology, and scholasticism.

Voltaire, who had attended the state funeral of Newton in 1727, wrote that this giant of science had "the particular good fortune, not only to be born in a country of liberty, but in an age when all scholastic impertinences were banished from the world. Reason alone was cultivated and humanity could only be its pupil." This judgment of Voltaire contributed much to propose Newton as a certain model of the scientist typical of the Age of Enlightenment. In the name of Reason, empirical sciences would now advance unfettered, freed from any animistic interpretation of the universe.[3]

No one today denies the benefit of distinguishing the realm of inductive science from that of philosophical or theological reflection. But in the name of pure reason, distinguishing methods soon meant opposition, and the relations between disciplines ended up in a state of bitter divorce. In its most radical rejection of tradition, science could not avoid the pitfall of reductionism. Scientism went so far as to profess that the only valid knowledge comes exclusively from the inductive method of natural sciences. This applied also to human beings and our highest values and ideals—love, for instance. Jean Rostand wrote, "the whole edifice of human love . . . is constructed upon the minimum molecular differences among a few derivatives of phenanthrene (estrogen and testosterone). . . . The so-called act of the will appears reducible to a pattern of coordinated reflexes . . . no less under compulsion than the caterpillar creeping toward the light."[4]

In all disciplines, even in human sciences, the same reductionism appeared in an effort to explain the origin of culture as the result of deterministic factors. Claude Lévi-Strauss affirms it quite explicitly: "I believe the ultimate call of the human sciences to be not to constitute, but to dissolve man. . . . [It is] incumbent on the exact natural sciences: the reintegration of culture in nature and, finally, of life within the whole of its physico-chemical conditions."[5]

Today, representatives of traditional cultures, aware of the contribution of modern sciences, cannot but wonder at the intellectual narrowness that ultimately brings about the destruction of humankind's capacity for universal knowledge, transcendence, and spiritual insight. Behind much of western anthropology's thinking there was a latent complex of superiority and a blinding ethnocentrism. The great cultures of the East were systematically downgraded. Thomas Macauley, a British historian of the nineteenth century, maintained that a single shelf of a good European library was worth the whole native literature of India and Arabia. He wrote: "It is, I believe, no exaggeration to say that all the historical information which has been collected from all the books written in the Sanskrit language is less valuable than what may be found in the most paltry abridgements used at preparatory schools in England. ..." He discouraged the training of specialists in Arabic and Sanskrit, whom he accused of spreading "artificial absurdity in history, in metaphysics, in physics and theology."[6]

A widespread opinion viewed the scientist as an objective researcher who must put aside everything but the subject under study, in order to be a cold observer, concentrated on his abstractions, insensitive to value judgments or even to the practical consequences of his discoveries. This attitude was inculcated as a strict ideal for the future scientist. Sociologist R. MacIver recalled, for instance, that if a researcher worked on a new explosive, he should not be worried if his discovery would actually be used to dig wells or tunnels or to improve firepower in wars.

## A SECOND LOOK AT THE MOTIVES OF SCIENTISTS

Today, a definite shift is taking place in the image of the scientist. The sociology of sciences and studies in the psychology of scientists[7] have shown that the attitudes of scientists are much more complex than many claimed they were. Their known motives and their behavior reveal the real drives that inspire their work.

Newton, for instance, is far from being the rationalist empiricist, as many claimed, arguing that in the vast amount of his publications no more than thirty pages or so referred to theological matters. A closer analysis of his manuscripts made public after 1936 has revealed an enormous amount of writings on questions dealing with God, Holy Scripture, spiritual and ethical problems. In fact, thanks to recent research on Newton and his unpublished writings, we discover a man quite different from the stereotype painted in the current textbooks.[8] We find, for example, that no less than eight thousand pages of his manuscripts were dedicated to religion. Newton, who was born on Christmas Day, thought of himself as chosen by God for a particular mission. The natural sciences, he admitted, do not lead us directly to the First Cause and to the Creator, but they bring us as close as possible in this earthly life. Through natural philosophy, as he wrote, "the bounds of moral philosophy will also be enlarged."[9] Newton had a keen sense of tradition, and he knew that he owed all to his predecessors, as he said in his famous expression, "We stand on the shoulders of giants and therefore we can see further."

This vision of science that combines empirical observation and spiritual insight has not been lost, and many examples can be found among the greatest of the modern names of science, who were also familiar with classical humanism. Einstein used to recall the list of authors that he liked to read with his fellow students; among them were Plato, Spinoza, Hume, Ampère, Poincaré, and also the Greek and French classics. For Einstein, science could not be cut off from art and from an experience of beauty and mystery of reality: "The most beautiful and most profound experience that man can have is the sense of the mysterious. This constitutes the foundation of religion and of all profound striving in art and science. He who has not experienced it seems to me — if not dead — at least blind."[10]

Similar attitudes are observed in other well-known scientists. What primarily drove Henri Poincaré in his research was not its practical usefulness but a sense of beauty and contemplation: "The scientist does not study nature because it is useful to do so. He studies it because he takes pleasure in it, and he takes pleasure in it because it is beautiful. If nature were not beautiful, it would not be worth knowing, and life would not be worth living."[11] Another illuminating example is found in a conversation between Bohr and Heisenberg, who were discussing why they had become quantum physicists, and quite famous at that, as we know. Bohr summed it up by saying that the initial impulse came from a sheer sense of admiration: "For me the starting point was the stability of matter which, from the standpoint of physics, is a pure wonder."[12] The same kind of admiration and veneration is expressed by Max Planck, who compared the joy of scientific discovery to that of the inspired poet: "He will find his satisfaction and inner happiness, as our great poet Goethe, in the knowledge that he has explored the explorable and quietly venerates the inexplorable."[13]

These examples, and many others that could be mentioned, show that the representation of scientists as pure rationalists, closed in a narrow ethical universe, can be quite misleading. It is true that these kinds of scientists have existed and still exist, but they are far from being the model.

The greatest among them seem to have been compassionate individuals dedicated as much to objective empirical research as to deep human and spiritual concerns. One could even say that a profound passion for science is intimately related to religious pursuit. As Einstein puts it:

> You will find among the profounder scientific minds scarcely one without a religious feeling of his own. . . . His religious feeling takes the form of rapturous amazement at the harmony of natural law, which reveals an intelligence of such superiority that, compared with it, all the systematic thought and action of human beings is an utterly insignificant reflection.[14]

Einstein was also well known for his deep social commitments, or as he calls it, "my passionate sense of social justice and social responsibility."[15]

One might add that the absence of such a spiritual and moral commitment can generate in some scientists a sense of real anguish. Many of them, who hardly see anything valid outside of empirical sciences, come to realize the fragile state of mind that results from their assumption. Science, they fear, will become a tyrant to humanity, the power of knowledge will destroy the power of love. As Bertrand Russell put it: "The scientific society of the future, as we have been imagining it, is one in which the power impulse has completely overwhelmed the impulse of love and this is the psychological source of the cruelties which it is in danger of exhibiting."[16]

## MATURING FACTORS IN SCIENTISTS' ETHICAL OUTLOOK

Maybe rational thinking would not have been sufficient by itself to achieve a desirable and necessary change, but recent and dramatic events have prompted a radical transformation in the way scientists tend to consider their moral responsibility and their commitment to the common good of the human family. Worldwide public opinion has now put the scientific world to an inexorable test. The production and actual use of the atom bomb has provoked a real trauma in the collective conscience of humankind, which for the first time has realized that it can be totally destroyed, with all the creations of civilizations. Everyone knows that, since Hiroshima and Nagasaki, the destructive power of modern weapons has increased to a saturation point. The consequence is almost unbearable for our minds and hearts: we live with a feeling of fear and doom that few periods in history have ever experienced.

How can honest scientists pretend to ignore the impact of their inventions and techniques on the lives and security of entire populations, on the integrity of nature, and on the biological and psychological balance of human beings? No one can escape the hard and painful challenges regarding our future and our survival. The development of futurology as a new discipline is one sign, among others, of our worried search about the fate that awaits us all.

Numerous prestigious associations of scientists in all fields have now put ethical problems high on their agendas. Questions touching fundamental issues such as life, death, peace, ecology, development, basic biological, cultural, and spiritual needs have become the common preoccupation of every man and woman of good will, including the scientist.

Gerald Holton has listed a number of important ethical and human values currently discussed by well-known professional associations of physicists and chemists: the access to science of underprivileged groups and countries, the right to oppose immoralpractices in research, the freedom of research in totalitarian countries, the sharing of scientific resources with poorer countries, and the effective means to achieve peace and disarmament.[17]

If today's scientists seem less involved than before in philosophical discussions about empirical and rational knowledge, they presently are much more interested in another branch of philosophy, namely ethics. As in the time of Socrates and the scholars of the seventeenth century, issues are now discussed about the relation between science and spiritual progress.[18]

Moreover, a great sense of moral responsibility has developed among scientists because of the fact that, as a social category, they have become a new power in society. The scientific sector, as it is called, carries much political weight in orienting government policies in the fields of industry, agriculture, medicine, education, administrative methods, and especially defense. Political debate between scientific groups and public opinion has become very lively, especially in questions relating to atomic energy, weapons, bio-engineering, and the protection of environment. These problems are now being raised in all countries by people of all classes and social conditions, and they have generated among scientists a new sense of corporate responsibility.

Another evolution is to be noted which is important for our purpose: ethnocentrism in science has largely been replaced by a new sense of internationalism. The wide circulation of major journals, the practice of regular conventions, the multiplication of international research projects, and the ongoing exchanges of experts between laboratories or universities have created a new sense of communal spirit among scientists everywhere in the world. The "invisible college" idea now takes a wider and more inclusive meaning.

## TOWARD A COMMON CODE OF UNIVERSAL VALUES

The shift in scientists' attitudes that we have just described is evidently to be interpreted more as a trend than as a definite acquisition. If the change is typical, it concerns only a minority, because many scientists still behave as technicians little interested in idealistic problems, as they say. Many are involved in research related to war and defense, without seeming to be disturbed much by what they consider, in practice, nontechnical questions. But it is a true sign of the times that in scientific quarters a larger and larger place is reserved to societal and ethical concerns. A new sense of accountability to the public is growing among experts. New forms of private and public controls, and also the pressure of better-informed populations, effectively remind the scientists of their responsibility and liability.

Could it be that we are witnessing the emergence of an ethical covenant intervening between science and society? In fact, scientific innovations have contributed to reunite the human family by improving communications, transportation, mobility, economic and cultural exchange among all peoples. As a consequence, humankind is consciously becoming ever more aware of its unity, of its rights, of its aspirations, of its common responsibility, and of its justified appeal to the conscience of experts. On the other hand, more and more scientists and scholars are sensitized to the service they owe to the human family they have helped bring together. This enlightened dialogue between the scientific sector and the public has to be recognized as a new dimension of modern culture.

A universal plea is now directed to all scientists by ordinary citizens of the world, who appear to be saying: Men and women of science, you represent a moral power never attained before by your colleagues. May your energy be mobilized for the just development of all peoples, starting with the poorest. The scientific and technical know-how exists to achieve that goal, but political will is lacking. Do bring the weight of your prestige to promote the development of all men and women, to defend the human rights of all. May your cooperation and moral commitment, while operating legitimately for the security of peoples, contribute effectively in building a culture of peace in the world. Few other groups can command such power, if consciously assumed, in order to foster intercultural understanding and universal brotherhood.

We all realize that, for the first time in history, the human being as such is becoming problematic. The very meaning of life is being dramatically questioned in the consciences of all, because all human life and all cultures could be wiped out by the decision of one of us capable of launching the nuclear holocaust. We all wish to refuse and reject this fatalistic outcome, not daring to believe the words of Claude Lévi-Strauss: "the world began without man and will end up without him." Never before have we understood so clearly that our common future depends on our common moral cooperation. Only wisdom will save us. Science, which is the new and real wealth of nations, now has to become an ally in serving this humanistic view of our future and growth.

Considering the role of science in building the future society, there is room for confidence. Many men and women are now cultivating research with a new holistic approach: they care about totality, universality, and transcendence. A new humanism is expressing itself in redefining intellectual approaches to reality. It defends a few basic principles: specialization can be reconciled with an interest for global problems; empirical research does not invalidate ethical pursuits; scientific abstraction does not eliminate compassion; identification with one's culture does not cut us off from other civilizations.

## FROM EAST AND WEST: SCIENCE AND WISDOM

This last point deserves special attention. I refer here to recent and inspiring efforts that are now taking place in overcoming the ethnocentric perspective of too many Western scholars. Many of them are now rediscovering with interest and admiration how much European science and technology owe to the Eastern civilizations. An international conference held in Venice in March 1986, whose proceedings have been published by UNESCO, has abundantly and aptly illustrated the debt of

Western science toward South Asia, India, China, Arabia, and Persia.[19] The cultural and scientific influence of these countries on the West has been demonstrated in many fields of knowledge: medicine, architecture, navigation, arithmetic, algebra, trigonometry, astronomy, botanical taxonomy, chemistry, physics, metallurgy — and also the major fields of human sciences, law, psychology, pedagogy, and philosophy. Plato, Pythagoras, and Parmenides, it is now recognized, were influenced directly and indirectly by the cultures of India. Through Greece and Rome, Europeans have been in contact with the contributions of the Arabs, of South Asia, and of China. As pleasantly noted by Donald Lach, when Matteo Ricci and the Jesuits came to China in the seventeenth century, bringing with them Western knowledge, their science in fact included arithmetic, algebra, and trigonometry, largely inspired by India, and also astronomy and cosmology originating from Hindu, Chinese, and Arab traditions.[20]

This ongoing dialogue between scientists from East and West seems to be a promise of mutual growth. It stimulates a new intellectual outlook regarding the past and future of science. It will help all of us to promote the rise and contribution of scientists from all parts of the world, not only from the Western countries and Japan. Should not India, for instance, play a greater role, considering that, according to the number of its scientific experts, it ranks third in the world? What about Chinese scientists and those that are emerging in Africa? How can they become full members of the scientific community without feeling alienated or overly dependent on their Western colleagues? There remains for all scientists, Eastern or Western, a problem of vast ethical and cultural dimensions. How can Asian and African scientists play in their own country the hard game of empirical science and technology, without the negative fallout that was experienced in the West, a form of industrialization and urbanization accompanied by materialism, hedonism, and the destruction of the natural and cultural environment? How can they cultivate modern science and also bring to the scientific community the humanistic patrimony of their cultures?

Thanks to these new lines of thought, science is now seen as including in itself a dynamic concern for ethics, for service, and for intercultural understanding. The spirit of interdisciplinarity is helping all of us to understand modern science as one of the paths toward the knowledge of all realities, material or immaterial, toward the contemplation of all truth and beauty.

A new dialogue is developing between scientists and traditional religions from East and West, with a better insight into the specific methods of respective fields of research. Religious leaders see more clearly today that the holy scriptures and traditions did not offer scientific views about the material constitution of the universe or about its astronomical structure. Scientists now realize better that they had often rejected not only the old religious cosmogonies, but also the universal message of wisdom contained in religious traditions and scriptures. Louis Pasteur used to say, *"peu de science éloigne de Dieu, beaucoup y ramène"* (a bit of science takes one away from God, a lot of science brings one back).

Well-known scientists are questioning the laws of determinism as an ultimate explanation for the constitution of physical reality and biological structure. The factors of order, organization, and information that transcend sheer probability and are at work to produce physical and biological regularities appear to postulate the existence of a Universal Intelligence, a transcendent Consciousness. With all due respect to the distinction of methods, many scientists come to realize that profound inquiry into the mystery of nature is not so far away from the reflections of theologians about creation.[21] Changes in attitudes are taking place among representatives of science and those of religion. This is precisely what has happened in the Catholic Church, when Pope John Paul II asked for a thorough revision of the Galileo affair, requesting that a special Commission report to him on the case, which it did in 1992.[22]

Is it not paradoxical today that in view of powerful and at times irrational and anti-scientific movements, the great religions, and the Catholic Church in particular, are among the first to defend the dignity and the necessity of intellectual research and philosophy as indispensable ways in discovering the secrets of the universe and the mystery of the human being?[23]

## SCIENCE AND THEOLOGY CONVERGING?

Scientists and theologians are coming to realize that the future of civilization will depend on their honest and courageous dialogue. If theologians recognize that their discipline is deeply challenged by the development of contemporary science, so it is with scientists who discover that their findings tend to raise inescapable problems about ultimate values such as truth and the meaning of human life. Both theologians and scientists have been encouraged by John Paul II to enter into this necessary and promising dialogue:

> Is the community of world religions, including the Church, ready to enter into a more thorough-going dialogue with the scientific community, a dialogue in which the integrity of both religion and science is supported and the advance of each is fostered? Is the scientific community now prepared to open itself to Christianity, and indeed to all the great world religions, working with us all to build a culture that is more humane and in that way more divine? Do we dare to risk the honesty and the courage that this task demands? We must ask ourselves whether both science and religion will contribute to the integration of human culture or to its fragmentation. It is a single choice and it confronts us all.[24]

Science and theology operate on very different levels of meanings and methods, yet they do converge in their complementary contributions to human progress. Not only theology but science also is potentially concerned with broader human culture which encompasses ultimate meanings and absolute values. Scientists who are open to the full implication of their search for total reality will acknowledge the common interests they share with theologians and philosophers. In the words of John Paul II:

> Scientists cannot, therefore, hold themselves entirely aloof from the sorts of issues dealt with by philosophers and theologians. By devoting to these issues something of the energy and care they give to their research in science, they can help others realize more fully the human potentialities of their discoveries. They can also come to appreciate for themselves that these discoveries cannot be a genuine sub-

stitute for knowledge of the truly ultimate. Science can purify religion from error and superstition; religion can purify science from idolatry and false absolutes. Each can draw the other into a wider world, a world in which both can flourish.[25]

A pressing recommendation appears to emerge from these considerations. There is an urgent need for all of us to promote an interdisciplinary dialogue, an interreligious and intercultural exchange, in order to bring about a new ethical consciousness capable of grasping the gravity of our common problems that have become a dramatic challenge to all the human family. In the final analysis, this is a call for hope that requires both great competence and wisdom.

# 6

# Christians and the Modern Conception of Cultural Rights

Central to the Church's dialogue with modern society is her strong commitment to defend the future of human culture. Modernity, as we have seen, undoubtedly represents an historic advance for humanity, but it also raises a radical challenge to our common survival as persons and societies. The crucial choices our generation has to face are in the order of higher values and ethical options. Therefore the specific contribution of the Church to modern society concerns the human conscience, and this belongs to the realm of culture. To all people of good will, Christians are called upon to announce the evangelical values that are at the root of human dignity and freedom. We are convinced that the future of the human being depends on culture, which means a civilized way of living together.

Viewed in this perspective, culture appears as a *basic right* for every man and woman. Without that right, human dignity is simply illusory. This insight is not new, but it takes on further significance in the context of the current debate about cultural development and human rights. Recent studies on human rights of the "third generation"[1] now include culture as a basic right for all. The difficulty is to know how cultural rights can be defended and effectively promoted.

To understand the complex issue of cultural rights, let us start with a very concrete question: Can a child born in a poor country of Africa legitimately aspire to a comparable cultural development that is normal for a young Westerner from a wealthy family? Is the situation of these two young people comparable in relation to their *right* to profit from the achievements of science, art, civilization? From the perception we have today of human rights, we are inclined to respond affirmatively to the question posed above. But our answer will have to consider the specific nature and origin of cultural rights. The right to share in "cultural riches" or "cultural goods" presents a problem *sui generis* that needs examining. The relation between culture and law constantly brings up new questions, as shown by the rare attempts to systematize national cultural policies and the jurisprudence concerning culture.[2] We will consider the question from a dual point of view, from that of ethics and that of political rights. This allows us to observe the progressive evolution of social thought and of the jurisprudence concerning cultural rights. Let us begin from the political aspect.

## POLITICAL RIGHTS

On the political plane itself, the main point to stress is that culture appears today as a right of a citizen corresponding to an obligation of the State. Traditionally, common law grants artists or writers an inalienable right to their works. In the same way, the holder of cultural goods or works of art has the right of possession guaranteed by law.

In modern times, the problem of cultural rights has considerably expanded in a twofold way. On the one hand, the notion of culture that was formerly limited to the intellectual, humanistic, or artistic dimension has now acquired a socio-historical meaning that embraces the distinctive characteristics of a human group and all the rights relative to its cultural identity. Moreover, precisely in view of this enlarged perception of cultural life, the modern State has come to consider culture as the object of its own policy. This evolution has been slow, but its developments are enlightening.

At the beginning stage, the State had the responsibility "not to inhibit freedom," or "not to limit" it. For example, the French Declaration of the Rights of Man and of the Citizen (1789) declares: "The free expression of thoughts and of opinions is one of man's most precious rights. Every citizen, therefore, can speak, write, and print freely, subject to answering for the abuse of freedom in the cases determined by law" (Art. 11).

This fundamental liberalism inspires as well the laissez-faire policy in the cultural matter of countries, as in the United States, which does not have an official cultural policy. It presupposes that the individual must be left free to express, perfect, and cultivate oneself according to one's potential and means. Culture, it is believed, will result from free initiative and free competition. There are merits in this position; it stimulates initiative and stresses the free condition of cultural activity. The criticism of this thesis is that it allows for grave cultural inequalities among large segments of the population, even in the most wealthy countries. Only those who already possess a minimum of instruction and know-how will effectively benefit from the available cultural advantages. Thus poor cultural minorities tend to perpetuate themselves.

In Europe, a different course has prevailed. After the Second World War, a more interventionist orientation of the State in the cultural domain became standard. Without dwelling too much on the experience of the Eastern countries — where governments before 1989 tended to mix Marxist ideology with the official culture — the countries of Western Europe, working through the Council of Europe that gradually was opened up to the countries of the East, developed a common thought and practice on policies dealing with cultural matters. They attributed to public authorities a positive responsibility for defending cultural rights and for the promotion of the cultural development of every citizen and of every group in the nation.Today most European governments have a Ministry for Cultural Affairs or an equivalent department dealing with culture. More than 125 countries in the world follow that pattern for their cultural policy.[3]

The United Nations, and above all UNESCO, have contributed considerably to the maturation of a universal consciousness in the area of cultural rights, cultural policies, and cultural development. This is especially the case with the Declaration of Mexico on Cultural Policies (1982) and the World Decade of

Cultural Development (1988-1997), to which we will return shortly.

## INTERNATIONAL STRUCTURES FOR CULTURAL RIGHTS

Among the most important international structures having to do with cultural rights, we must mention the *Universal Declaration of Human Rights* adopted by the United Nations in 1948, which formally stipulated the right to education and culture. It stressed that education is to be seen as "the full development of the human personality," directed toward understanding and peace (Art. 26). Especially notable is Article 27, which even more clearly relates to culture: "(1) Everyone has the right to freely participate in the cultural life of the community, to enjoy the arts and to share in scientific advancement and its benefits. (2) Everyone has the right to the protection of moral and material interests resulting from any scientific, literary or artistic production of which he is the author."

In 1966, the United Nations adopted an *International Covenant on Economic, Social and Cultural Rights*. This pact constitutes for the signatory States a juridical obligation, and not just a moral directive, as in the Declaration of 1948. Article 15 sets down the cultural rights of each person: "The States Parties to the present Covenant recognize the right to everyone: a) to take part in cultural life; b) to enjoy the benefits of scientific progress and its applications; c) to benefit from the protection of the moral and material interests resulting from any scientific, literary or artistic achievement of which he is the author." The States made themselves responsible, moreover, to take the necessary measures to assure "the conservation, the development and the diffusion of science and culture," and to facilitate "international co-operation in the scientific and cultural fields" (Art. 15).

In the *Declaration on the Right to Development* of 1986, the United Nations enlarged the meaning of cultural rights, in the sense that these became equated with the rights of the "third generation." The Declaration establishes a certain solidarity among civil, economic, and cultural rights: all these rights are considered as "indivisible." Article 6 underlines it in this way: "equal attention and urgent consideration should be given to the implementation, promotion and protection of civil, political, economic, social and cultural rights." This Declaration does not have any coercive power, and some specialists do not accept these collective rights, in that they lack precision, are difficult to enforce juridically, and there is the risk that they would conflict with the rights of the individual. Without entering into the legal debate, it is interesting to note the new interpretation this Declaration grants to the right for the total development of the person and of peoples: "The right of development is an inalienable human right by virtue of which every human person and all peoples are entitled to participate in, contribute to, and enjoy economic, social, cultural and political development, in which all the human rights and all fundamental freedoms can be fully realized" (Art. 1).

When one looks at the difference between the legal and moral plane, it is important to recognize the principle of universal solidarity, which is the foundation of a right to cultural development for all peoples. In addressing the International Labor Organization, Paul VI did not hesitate to affirm "the right, in solidarity, of peoples to their total development" (June 6, 1969). The same principle was taken up again by the United Nations when it launched the World Decade of Cultural Development (1988-1997).

The notion of cultural rights, as we can see, finds areas of application that are more and more vast: persons, nations, peoples in development, and the international community. A particularly significant application concerns the child. *The United Nations Convention on the Rights of the Child* addressed itself to this issue in 1989.

This Convention, in contrast to the Charter of 1959 called the *Declaration of the Rights of the Child*, is a legal instrument that has the force of law. Several educational and cultural aspects deserve to be stressed in this new Convention.

Children are guaranteed the right to express their views, taking into consideration their age and maturity (Art. 12), and to seek, receive, and impart information of all kinds, including art forms (Art. 13). The signatory States are responsible to protect the rights of the child to freedom of thought, conscience, and religion (Art. 14). They affirm the importance of the mass media as the transmitter of national and international culture in the first stages of a child's development. They encourage the production of "information and materials of social and cultural benefit to the child," as well as an exchange of such information and material, "from the diversity of cultural, national and international sources." The State systematically encourages the dissemination of children's books, asking that "the linguistic needs of the child who belongs to a minority group or who is indigenous" be taken into account (Art. 17). The Convention recalls the right of the disabled child to receive a true education, with the aim of achieving "the fullest possible social integration and individual development, including his or her cultural and spiritual development" (Art. 23).

## THE ETHICAL FOUNDATION OF CULTURAL RIGHTS

As the above overview demonstrates, the development of international rights invites a more general consideration of the fundamental ethics involved in cultural rights. The ethical presupposition for cultural rights is clearly observable in the concept of culture as presented by UNESCO in the Declaration of Mexico of 1982. There culture is so described. "It includes not only the arts and letters, but also modes of life, the fundamental rights of the human being, value systems, traditions and beliefs." Culture is a part of "the fundamental rights of the human being" precisely because it "gives man the ability to reflect upon himself ... (it) makes us specifically human, rational beings, endowed with a critical judgment and a sense of moral commitment."[4]

The right *to* culture and the right *of* culture is then a fundamental human right, prior to every positive law. If human beings realize themselves only through culture, then it follows that culture is a necessity of life and is just as urgent as the fundamental biological needs. It is the right to a really human life. This primary right is constitutive and forms the basis of the varied facets of cultural rights. It is impossible to enumerate all of these. Suffice it to mention, in particular, the right to education, to schooling, to a basic apprenticeship, to professional instruction; access to higher education, the right to work, to the practice of a profession, to a lifelong education; the right to the freedom of expression, information, and communication, to creative activity; the right to reputation, the right to a choice of life, the right to found a family, the right of association, the freedom to travel. A detailed list of these principal rights is found in John XXIII's encyclical *Pacem in Terris* (1963).

If we were to inquire as to the fundamental basis for the right to culture, we find it in the radical freedom of the human spirit, founded on the freedom of conscience, that renders each person responsible for his or her own destiny. Human beings can only grow through the search for meaning and in opening themselves to the Transcendent. Culture assures us of this indispensable spiritual freedom. The right to culture is essentially linked to religious freedom. John Paul II, in his encyclical *Centesimus Annus* (1991), explains it in this way: "In a certain sense, the source and synthesis of these rights is religious freedom, understood as the right to live in the truth of one's faith and in conformity with one's transcendent dignity as a person" (No. 47).

All these rights concern the person, but since there is a social aspect involved, it is hard to distinguish exactly between individual and collective rights. As to the latter, we must mention the right to an officially guaranteed national identity, the right to language, the rights of minorities, the right to cultural development, and the right for each people to be assured of the conditions for such development: namely, the infrastructures of an educational system, a network of free communication, a system of law, and the means for a policy concerning culture, cultural patrimony, and research.

## DOES DISTRIBUTIVE JUSTICE APPLY TO CULTURAL GOODS?

After having formulated the ethical principle that forms the basis of the human right to culture, we must now ask how cultural goods can actually be made accessible to individual persons and groups. The question refers to the universal destination of cultural riches. In a vastly interdependent world, how are we to understand the sharing of cultural goods by every person and all human groups? In other words, can the rules of distributive justice be applied in a strict sense to the realm of cultural goods and rights?

First of all, we have to clarify the communal character of cultural goods by remembering the nature of culture, its mode of acquisition and transmission. In this question concerning culture and ethics, our central reference is the good of the person, the first creator and beneficiary of cultural progress. From the perspective of the person, then, it is each human being who perfects himself or herself through schooling, intellectual training, the deepening of knowledge, and the creativity of the spirit. It is characteristic of a person whom we call cultured to know how to expand his or her talents. Certainly culture demands the transmission of knowledge, but it results from the basic effort toward self-mastery and self-perfection. It results from self-development and self-enrichment. As persons, we are the only ones capable of inner growth and maturation. No one else can take our place in this. We must recognize this singularity and nontransferability in the culture of every person. We are made aware of this when death takes a great teacher or famous artist from us. We have the feeling of an irretrievable loss to culture. Everyone distinguishes himself or herself by cultivating individual talents and by extending the knowledge and experience that have made them grow as a human being.

Let us add to this, however, that the authentic advancement of the person calls for, in return, a continual exchange in the midst of the human community; otherwise a self-satisfied encapsulation would lead to a spiritual death. What I know as personal acquisition is simultaneously the enrichment that I share with others. Science, art, and culture demand personal interiorization and collective exchange. Knowledge, know-how, and the style of life then become the attribute of individual persons as well as of the entire cultivated society. This value must be defended as an inalienable good and a right that characterizes both individuals and human groups.

## COMMON CULTURAL GOODS

Each human community defines itself by its culture, that is to say, by its original and unique way of seeing life, of judging it, of behaving, of viewing the arts, and of creating institutions that humanize the material and social realm. Culture understood in this way defines the identity of each human community. It is the highest value, the typical cultural heritage, and the plan of life that no society could sacrifice without destroying itself. Herein lies a fundamental right. But the culture of groups as well as persons cannot survive in isolation without the danger of impoverishment, of dehumanization, and of nonculture. The promotion of cultural identity, out of an inner need, calls for the understanding and the dialogue of cultures. This reciprocity underlines the interdependence of the cultural goods of each person and each group. One sees how much the universal destination of immaterial goods can be realized through a free exchange and reciprocal enrichment. In fact, it is the characteristic of cultural riches that we are able to share them without becoming poorer ourselves. Usually the contrary is the rule. When a culture spreads itself out, it is deepened and takes on a greater universal significance.

Human solidarity would be illusory without taking into consideration a dual need: first, that cultural enrichment become the proper wealth of each person and each society; second, that the mutual fertility of individual cultures becomes a source of continued enrichment to all human culture. A common cultural good is therefore becoming an imperative, and modern society is now made aware of this. Culture constitutes a real right, but it imposes at the same time a common obligation toward universal culture.

Confronted with the development of all persons and peoples, we can better understand the function of science, art, and culture in the progress of human society. New ethical problems are impinging on the universal conscience and on Christian thinking. Let us name a few of the more recent developments, summarizing them in the following terms: the socialization of science, the advance of cultural development, the politicizing and democratization of culture, and the universal extension of human rights comprising those of culture.

## SCIENCE, A SOCIETAL GOOD

Science is no longer only the business of individual savants. Science now constitutes a real institution of society. The scientific sector represents a considerable power that implicates men and women of science in the collective responsibility for the promotion of a just, peaceful, and fraternal society. Science has socialized itself, and research centers are now subject to the norms and rules of conduct dictated by the common good. A new right concerning science, its acquisition, and its application is taking shape.

The modern State has the task of defining a scientific policy, in order to give a nation a balanced tool in the main disciplines that are vital for the progress of industry, medicine, defense, basic research, and the quality of life. Let us note the growing role of the human sciences in this regard. Criteria for the mutual sharing of scientific progress call for an enlightened policy. The task becomes more complicated by the simple fact that science progresses rapidly, that knowledge accumulates almost unlimitedly, and that the disciplines are becoming super-specialized, creating often the objective fact of noncommunicability between experts and nonexperts. How then can society control the use of science for the benefit of all?

The international aspect of scientific policies poses problems still more complex. Allowing for the right to legitimate secrecy, the respect for the patenting of inventions, and authors' rights, how can the advantages of scientific discoveries effectively benefit all nations? The policy and the praxis of the rich nations in the areas of science and technology tends to create a new situation of dependence or even of cultural colonization. The sharing of scientific progress among nations needs much understanding and generosity on the part of the scientific world and of political leaders. Their responsibility is immense, in view of the challenges of development of all peoples.

## THE RIGHT TO CULTURAL DEVELOPMENT

The right to cultural development today stresses the humanist and ethical dimension in the progress of peoples. An authentic development demands the sharing of the economic and cultural accomplishments of human progress. Experience has amply demonstrated that development plans are deceiving or at least illusory, if they limit themselves to the economic or technical aspects, neglecting the identity of peoples and their cultural aspirations. No human group can progress at the price of losing its soul and its own culture. To profit from the positives of modernization, people in developing countries must make a very difficult choice. In accepting science and modern culture, they must discern those elements compatible with their traditional culture. Moreover, they must ask themselves what traditional values must be kept alive in a developing country to preserve its national identity.

The advantages of science and technology today have considerable importance in the development of nations, as John Paul II has noted: "In our time, in particular, there exists another form of ownership which is becoming no less important than land: the possession of know-how, technology and skill. The wealth of the industrialized nations is based much more on this kind of ownership than on natural resources."[5] The task of the industrially more advanced nations is to explore along with the developing countries ways to share technical know-how. Responsible decisions must be made on both sides. If these decisions are not made soon, there is the risk that the culture of the wealthy nations will blot out the culture of the developing countries. The latter aspire ardently to acquire all the advantages of science and cultural creativity, and certainly development programs should respond to this need. But it is only through a responsible dialogue between the rich and the poor countries that cultural cross-communication can respect the need to honor national identities and the free sharing of the values of education, science, and art which should gradually become the common patrimony of humanity. It must be added that this patrimony equally includes the wealth of customs, artistic heritage, the wisdom and philosophy of traditional cultures.

From now on, these needs require nations to formulate their own cultural policy. The minimum objective is to defend and promote the common cultural patrimony of the nation: sites, monuments, traditional and popular art, archives, literary and artistic works. A more ambitious goal is increasingly more apparent: it is directed toward cultural democratization, according to which all citizens and groups should potentially have access to the advantages of science, education, art, and a continuing education. This is a right that is now being recognized as belonging to citizens of the modern State.

## CULTURE AND UNIVERSAL JUSTICE

The balance between cultural identity and the interdependence of cultures is not easily realizable. How can each person and each group remain faithful to its own identity when taking on the culture of others? This is an acute problem for immigrants and minorities.

A real universalization of culture can legitimately be pursued, given the growing interdependence of all nations. Justice demands, however, that the distinctive traits of each culture be protected and promoted, otherwise the danger of standardization of cultures arises. Certainly, the advantages of science, technology, and art can contribute to the progress of all persons and groups, but the effective sharing of these advantages should be obtained through a free exchange among the parties concerned. If this fundamental right is not recognized, the law of the strongest becomes the norm, as is unfortunately the case in situations of cultural colonization and imperialism.

The free sharing of all in the advantages of culture has to do with universal justice. Today the principle is commonly admitted, even if the application of this principle reveals itself to be extremely complex, precisely because of the nature of cultural goods and their mode of acquisition.

We return then to our central question: Does distributive justice apply in the sharing of cultural goods? Perhaps, but in a special way. Cultural goods cannot be distributed as material goods. It is not simply a question of sharing the sum of knowledge and artistic achievement among all, but rather of rendering each person intellectually capable of receiving in total freedom the treasures of knowledge, science, and art. We are speaking here of a higher justice, of a fundamental right permitting all men and women to fulfill themselves as human beings. To benefit from cultural goods, education is necessary first, followed by an ongoing initiation that requires time, application, and much effort. This is a task that never ends, for the treasures of human culture, including those of theology and sacred art, are inexhaustible. Immense ethical progress could be accomplished if people today were convinced that all the resources of science and art must continually contribute to the intellectual and spiritual elevation of all men and women. This is a requirement of justice and equity that modern law is seeking to formulate.

As we can see, the international community is giving a much wider interpretation to the rights and corresponding obligations concerning the sharing of all in cultural advantages. The juridical import of the official conventions will undoubtedly be drafted with more precision, so that little by little the requirements of ethics will be met. The objective has been clearly formulated in the words of Paul VI: "the equal distribution of the wealth of nature and of the fruits of civilization."[6] In view of the vocation of all to pursue cultural growth, which is never optional for anyone, the social teaching of the Church strongly stresses tight-knit solidarity among human beings. The Church plays a specific role in cultural growth, for it goes to the heart of cultural reality, that is, the human heart. All are called to grow interiorly, to develop themselves in solidarity, and to transcend themselves. In *Centesimus Annus*, John Paul II has illustrated the aspiration of all toward cultural development, and he has shown the Church's way of serving authentic culture:

> For an adequate formation of a culture, the involvement of the whole man is required, whereby he exercises his creativity, intelligence, and knowledge of the world and of people. Furthermore, he displays his capacity for self-control, personal sacrifice, solidarity and readiness to promote the common good. Thus the first and most important task is accomplished within man's heart. The way in which we are involved in building our own future depends on the understanding we have of ourselves and of our own destiny. It is on this level that *the Church's specific and decisive contribution to true culture* is to be found.[7]

## A FUTURE PERSPECTIVE

As Christians, we reaffirm that all human persons, participating in God's own creativity, have the elemental right to culture, which allows them personal growth according to their talents, aptitudes, and aspirations. This is why cultural rights today are recognized as an integral part of human rights. The international community and the States, in becoming aware of this, are searching to interpret cultural rights through binding legal statements and policies for the advantage of the cultural development of all persons and groups. The realization of these objectives presupposes, therefore, that the particular conditions for the effective sharing of cultural advantages be respected. To truly activate their cultural rights, persons must be motivated, supported institutionally, and become apt for growth on an intellectual, moral, and spiritual plane.

The enforcement of these rights will require an all-out solidarity throughout the world. The Church plays a specific role in making us aware that solidarity is really an indispensable virtue for the total development of persons and peoples. John Paul II brought this out clearly in his encyclical *Sollicitudo Rei Socialis*,[8] which can be read as a major document on cultural development.

Seen from a Christian perspective, the cultural growth of persons and groups is not only pursued through the enforcement of rights. It is, first of all, the fulfillment of a basic aspiration that can be realized only through a change of attitude by the whole of society. A true cultural conversion will be needed. A new evangelization of mentalities will be indispensable. The "power of the Gospel" will have to be applied to achieve this kind of cultural change toward the Christianization of the world.

Christians nowadays are becoming aware that the universal realization of cultural rights will remain a dream unless certain ethical and spiritual conditions are met in society. This concerns human rights in general, which have been effectively proclaimed by international bodies, but which in practice are meeting profound cultural resistance in many parts of the world. Westerners have too hastily taken human rights for granted, as if they were a universal and undisputed conquest. This appears to have been largely a projection of the Western mind, and some say an imposition of our worldview. Recent studies on the cultural foundations of human rights[9] have shown to what extent these modern rights have been influenced by Western culture, by the

Enlightenment, the Reformation, the Counter-Reformation, the American Constitution, the French Declaration on the Rights of Man, by the legal experience of modern States, and by the social doctrines comprising the Church's teaching. Other cultural traditions, such as the Indian, Hindu, Islamic, Buddhist, Confucian, the African animist, and the pre-Columbian cultures, do not spontaneously share our concept of the person, the State, central authority, separation of powers, democratic control, equality, freedom, and accountability of the individual, which are prerequisites for a human rights system. These cultures have other views of the relationships of persons with communities, with nature, with the world, and with the divine. Let us add that the full acceptance of human rights, including cultural rights, is far from being an unqualified success in industrialized countries, where disturbing injustices are generated by structures that tolerate what has been called "new poverty," discrimination, technological unemployment, ethnic divisions, and the marginalization of minorities and migrants. What cultural rights do these people enjoy in reality? The conquest of cultural rights remains partial, indeed.

Sociological research now shows that our concept of human rights is intimately linked to a Jewish and Christian vision of persons, human communities, divine authority, and the transcendent destiny of human beings, values not always explicitly acknowledged. This brings us again to our main purpose, which is the evangelization of modernity as a culture. The realm of human rights, and of cultural rights in particular, represents an immense field where Christians have a specific responsibility to promote Gospel values, which now appear more clearly as the spiritual and moral prerequisites for the defense of human rights in all societies and cultures. Justice and culture cannot but grow together.

# 7

# The New Evangelization Facing Agnostic Culture

Confronted with modern unbelief, the Church has developed a new approach since Vatican II. There is a keen awareness that unbelief today is tantamount to a *new culture*, and it is to this culture that the Gospel must speak.

In the past, unbelief was primarily considered from its philosophical, individual, and moral perspectives. Atheism was the offspring of certain currents of thought and theories of the human being, human origins, and human destiny. There was, at the same time, the atheism of those who reject God or of those who simply dismiss him from their lives. These forms of unbelief still exist, and Christians cannot ignore them in the work of evangelization.

## UNBELIEF BECOMES A CULTURE

The new, dramatic element of our time is the fact that unbelief, especially in the form of widespread religious indifference, has become a culture. Unbelief is no longer merely a matter of ideas or personal attitudes leading to a rejection of God. We now confront a difficult cultural phenomenon. This is a psycho-

---

Translated by Robert R. Barr

social fact, and it has to be analyzed as such. Unbelief corresponds to a life-style that has spread throughout all modern societies and become the habitual way of life of millions of people. God has been quietly canceled off the list of their dominant values and from their ordinary mode of thinking, communicating, working, and doing business. If questioned, many will claim they can do without God. It does not make any difference in their life. In traditional societies, every human activity had a religious reference, at least potentially. The contrast with today's culture is striking. Everything that counts in secularized society is simply a-religious in character. The religious dimension is absent from modern institutions, models of behavior, currents of thought, social, economic, and cultural affairs. Our society today functions without God. In the eyes of many, the return of the religious element would actually represent an act of anti-cultural sectarianism, so they urge us peacefully to keep God away. For vast sectors of the population, religion is strictly a private affair. In this view, any attempt to insert religious values into modern culture would be regarded as unwarranted proselytism. The tranquil assumption is that a modernized society should operate on a God-less basis. This is a common tenet of an advanced secular culture.

Proclaiming Jesus Christ to this new culture is the major challenge of evangelization today. We face a formidable temptation to resign ourselves to a culture that gives all the signs of being satisfied and solidly ensconced in its religious void. Does the pressing admonition and call of Saint Paul, "Woe to me if I do not preach the Gospel" (1 Cor. 9:16) really apply to our times? Of course, Christians can never shy away and forget St. Paul's cry. No culture is cut off from the grace of the Savior of all peoples. One of the most difficult tasks of the Church will now be to understand this present culture, search out its hidden expectations, and find a new way to bring to it the message of Christ. The future of the Church in modern society is at stake. Christians today are becoming ever more aware that the new field for evangelization is this secularized culture. Culture itself has to be evangelized, that is, the conscience of persons as well as the collective conscience of modern societies.

When evangelizers embrace this perspective, they are confronted with the spiritual drama of our times. They collide with the opacity of cultures, which screens out the Gospel. It is as if the message of Jesus Christ made no impression upon modern mentalities. Moral and areligious subjectivism tends to become the dominant attitude of secularized cultures. We now seem to have entered a post-Christian era. The Gospel has to be announced anew to the era we have now entered. Hence, the conviction that culture as such must become the target of a new evangelization. It is no longer enough to reach persons one by one, however indispensable this might be. The power of the Gospel must now reach and transform mentalities and cultures themselves.[1]

## CULTURE: A HUMAN REALITY TO BE EVANGELIZED

Some find it difficult to enter into the perspective of evangelizing cultures. Their objection runs: Is not evangelization addressed exclusively to persons—who alone are capable of making an act of faith and being converted to the ideal of the Gospel? Surely we have to recognize that only the individual conscience is capable of listening to the call of Jesus and of eliciting the decisive actions that make one Christian. Only persons can be baptized, confirmed, absolved, and tend toward holiness throughout their lives. Therefore, there is no doubt that evangelizing means converting individual persons to Jesus Christ.

Yet, evangelization has a wider meaning: it achieves the Christianization not only of individuals but also of common patterns of behavior, traditions, mores, and institutions. The whole history of the Church testifies to the fact that the Gospel has created new cultures with their own unmistakable manifestations, such as schools of thought, art, Christian institutions, codes of law, and spiritual traditions that still influence the world. In the past, such an evangelizing process went on almost unobserved, because the pace of cultural change followed a generational or epochal rhythm. Today the whole process of cultural change has been radically precipitated. Instead of the slow cultural evolution of the past, present societies are thrown into an almost sudden change in values, ways of living, and institutions.

*Mind*

This cultural shock is now provoking in all people everywhere a sense of anguish and a shared questioning about our human future. Evangelization, we now realize, has to address this common state of mind in order to bring the answers of Jesus Christ to the crucial questioning of modern cultures. This has been the major concern of the Church since Vatican II.

We must get beyond a certain fatalism or passive resignation and face the challenge of new cultures—that is, the challenge of the mentalities, values, and types of behavior that spread throughout society and challenge our conception of the human being and Christian life. Modern culture, to be sure, has been the vehicle of immense progress, as we have shown in chapters 1 and 2. But like any other human reality, it must be enlightened, purified, and elevated by the spirit of the Gospel. Above all, those areas of culture need to be reached where God has been thrust aside or simply forgotten. In order to understand the meaning of this special kind of conversion, we must begin with the mental perception of culture as a human reality to be evangelized.

## EVANGELIZING BEHAVIOR MODELS

But how does one evangelize a culture? First of all, by discovering the dimensions of the culture that have an impact on collective thinking and acting, that constitute the *ethos* of a society. These dimensions are the typical behavior models of a given milieu, the criteria of judgment, the dominant values, the major interests, habits, and customs that influence work, leisure activities, and the experiences of family, social, economic, and political life. An ethos corresponds to the practical morality prevailing in a given milieu—the mind-set that so powerfully conditions behaviors. The ethos that guides many sectors of modern societies is inspired by an agnostic, materialistic, and utilitarian view of life. For example, some groups consider as "normal" uncontrolled experimentation on human beings, the domination of one race by another, slavery, infanticide, abortion, euthanasia, torture, or terrorism. To evangelize these groups will mean to discern, or denounce, those elements in a given culture that contradict the Gospel and ultimately assault the dignity of the human being.

We must perceive the areas that pose new ethical and spiritual problems. We must ask ourselves what is the sensitivity or mentality that characterizes the various sectors of society: the family, education, work, business, the media, minorities, the underprivileged, the young, the unemployed, the sick, and the marginalized. Any time we witness the yearning and suffering of the human heart, we should try to impart the word of the Gospel and the hope in Jesus Christ.

John Paul II continually repeats to Christians the world over this pressing invitation:

> You must help the Church to respond to these fundamental questions for the cultures of today: how is the message of the Church accessible to new cultures, to current forms of understanding and sensitivity? How can the Church of Christ make itself understood by the modern spirit, a spirit so proud of its achievements and at the same time so uneasy about the future of the human family? *Who is Jesus Christ* for the men and women of today?[2]

## TOWARD A SECOND EVANGELIZATION OF CULTURES

Today the task of evangelizing cultures is complicated by the fact that the people to be Christianized have already been touched by the message of Christ, but the Good News has faded into indifference or agnosticism. Bossuet said long ago, "There is an atheism hidden in all hearts, that spills out into all actions: God counts for nothing."[3] Secular society has aggravated the climate of inhibited or dormant faith. Thus, it is incumbent upon the Church to undertake a second evangelization. Let us ask ourselves what the difference is between the first and second evangelization.

The first evangelization reveals the novelty of Christ the Redeemer "to the poor," to set them free, convert them, baptize them, and implant the Church among them. Evangelization is propagated through the ordinary channels of Christian influence: family, parish, school, and communities of life. This is in itself an authentic evangelization of culture—that is, a Christianization of human mentalities, hearts, minds, and institutions. This is how traditional cultures have been Christianized, by a slow process of osmosis. The conversion of consciences has profoundly transformed institutions. We are familiar with the prototypes of the first evangelization: Saint Paul, Saint Irenaeus, Saint Patrick, Saints Cyril and Methodius, and Saint Francis Xavier.

A number of evangelizers of the past knew quite well how to carry on inculturation, long before the birth of the expression. John Paul II illustrated the penetration of the Gospel in the countries of Europe through a process of inculturation before the word existed, in particular among the Slav peoples: "Saints Cyril and Methodius anticipated gains that were only fully taken up by the Church with Vatican II—in the inculturation of the Gospel message within the various civilizations, by adopting the language, customs, and spirit of the race in their full value."[4] We shall also note that the first evangelization is far from finished in the world, and we see how difficult it often is in India, in Japan, in the Islamic and Buddhist cultures, and in many sectors of modern society that are cut off from religious values.

Let us now turn to the second evangelization, also called re-evangelization or new evangelization. The second or new evangelization is addressed to populations that have been Christianized in the past but which now live in a secularized climate, devaluing religion or combatting it, and marginalizing believers and their communities. This is an entirely new situation, never before experienced in the history of the Church.

What is needed is a common effort to identify the subjects or recipients of the new evangelization, an indispensable condition for the re-evangelization of persons and cultures.

## TO WHOM IS THE NEW EVANGELIZATION ADDRESSED?

Let us attempt to comprehend the mentality of the persons who are in need of the new evangelization.

## THE NOUVEAUX RICHES

These persons lack the attitude of the "poor of the Gospel." Rather they behave like the "rich," enjoying what they possess, self-satisfied, enclosed within their autonomy, comfort, and self-fulfillment. It is this collective mind-set that we must penetrate, with empathy, in order to expose its limits before the Absolute God. In this way, the spiritual poverty often hidden beneath an attitude of self-satisfaction or indifference can become evident.

## A FAITH THAT LACKS DEEP ROOTS

With many persons, their first faith has not developed for lack of roots or depth. Often the first evangelization has been insufficient, superficial, and has gradually lost its savor and died out for lack of interiorization and solid motivation. Faith has not been strengthened by a personal experience of Christ, by the sharing of faith in love and joy, nor has it been consolidated by the support of a close, living Christian community.

## A FAITH THAT IS REJECTED AND REPRESSED

Many nominal Christians, living in a state of indifference, have rejected religion because it represents for them a painful experience and is felt to be morally oppressive; their faith has remained at an infantile stage. Popular culture frequently confuses religion and moralism. This view of religion generates fear and acts on unconscious anxieties. For the sake of freedom, religion and the Church are then rejected as alienating. We must ask ourselves what shortcomings in the first evangelization could have provoked this perception of Christian faith.

## A FAITH THAT IS DORMANT

It is difficult to say of these persons that their faith is entirely dead. But it is asleep, inoperative, forgotten, covered over by other interests and concerns — money, well-being, comfort, pleasure — that often become real idols. In traditional Christian countries, the pressure of religious custom sustained the faithful and favored a regular sacramental practice. This social pressure does not necessarily invalidate traditional religious practice, which has produced great Christians. However, the new climate of indifference leaves people spiritually alone, face-to-face with themselves and their own responsibilities, which they often perceive in confusion. Disenchantment and spiritual uncertainty render the individual fragile, anguished, and open to credulity. Moral isolation makes persons sensitive to a kind word of welcome. The sects have often understood this better than we. We must carefully reexamine our psychological and spiritual method of evangelization.

## A CONSCIENCE THAT LACKS MORAL STRUCTURE

An even more disturbing phenomenon is a kind of "demoralization" that deprives a person of all moral or spiritual structure. It becomes almost impossible to make an act of faith when an individual mistrusts all ideology, all belief, any great commitment that requires one to transcend oneself. Some observers have noted this psychology as typical of modern fiction: the loss of any "moral center" or "moral concern." The tendency is aggravated when the individual retreats into a purely subjective autonomy. Modern society tends to exalt this individualistic attitude into a system. Sociologist Talcott Parsons has shown very well how this "institutionalized individualism" finally leads to "individualistic corruption."[5] We can easily surmise what a formidable obstacle the evangelizer must overcome in order to reach the conscience of such persons.

Despite the difficulties, we must convince ourselves that, in all hearts ultimately, there is a thirst for peace, a longing for enlightenment and happiness.

## A LATENT HOPE

The new evangelization requires as a first step that we grasp the anxieties and hopes of people around us. Have we really entered the spirit of the Vatican Council, which was so attentive to the mentality of our contemporaries? We must strive to understand the anguish hidden beneath the seemingly tranquil attitudes of people we meet. Never before, perhaps, has there been such a search for meaning—such a passionate quest for reasons for living. The awareness of this latent need for hope is essential in the process of evangelization. Beneath the anguish we have to perceive the positive aspirations that reveal themselves confusedly. Do we sufficiently appreciate the cultural aspirations of our age? Let us reflect on these values and aspirations that are so typical of our times: a sense of co-responsibility, of solidarity, of personal decision, of interiorization, of religious freedom, a new view of the laity's responsibility, of women's roles, of youth's aspirations, and the universal quest for justice, peace, and development for all human beings. We find these socio-pastoral preoccupations in all of the Council documents, and they are concrete concerns connected with evangelization. We should reread the documents of Vatican II from this perspective. A latent hope and spiritual thirst lie hidden in people's hearts. Our task is to catch the glimmer of hope present in our culture, in order to bring to it the Christian response.

## HOW TO RE-EVANGELIZE CULTURES?

### CULTURE IS NO LONGER AN ALLY

In the context of a second evangelization, the challenge is the new culture. There is no longer a "support culture," as there used to be in traditional societies. Today the Church confronts a culture of indifference or opposition. In some societies there is even persecution and oppression. Elsewhere there is stark disinterest, a calm elimination that relativizes all beliefs.

Yet a pluralistic culture, that puts all beliefs on the same level, can actually offer the evangelizer a new opportunity—a chance to make known our unique point of view within the chorus of opinions. We too can use to our advantage the modern means of influencing public opinion through proclaiming the novelty of our message. Special education for living and acting in a pluralistic culture is necessary for the future.

## DETECTING OBSTACLES TO THE NEW EVANGELIZATION

Obstacles to the new evangelization may vary greatly from one part of the world to another. In some countries of Christian traditions, the Church has been, as it were, disfigured by a slow erosion. Faith has been eliminated or rejected through a gradual process of secularization. This has engendered a culture of indifference, one of the most formidable obstacles to re-evangelization. Religion seems no longer relevant to an ever-growing mass of individuals who are spiritually "somewhere else" and who live in an a-religious universe.

The situation of unbelief differs widely from nation to nation. In a number of countries, re-evangelization is addressed to populations that painfully remember persecution, religious wars, revolutions, or atheistic government policies. Others have suffered foreign colonization, exploitation, or in the last century the loss of the faith among the working class. It is of the utmost importance that we understand the collective psychology at work in the historical experience of each group to be evangelized.

## PENETRATING THE WALL OF INDIFFERENCE

In Western countries, secularization has propagated a climate of religious indifference, of unbelief, or spiritual insensitivity. The Gospel is not entirely unknown or entirely new, and we find ourselves confronted dramatically with an ambiguous religious psychology. Faith is, as it were, both present and absent in people's minds and hearts. The salt of the Gospel has lost its savor. Even its *words* have lost their edge. The words *Gospel, Church, Christian faith* are no longer new. They have become worn, banal. The identification of culture as "Christian" has become superficial, as we see, for example, in the lot that has befallen the celebrations of Christmas and Easter, with the mundane commercialization of these feasts. Christian traditions have become conventionalized, a part of people's customs, like folklore or any cultural trait of a given milieu. We must react against a culturalization of Christianity that reduces it to secularized phenomena or non-sacral customs. Christians must make their treasure, "the pearl of great price," seem once more a thing of value in public opinion, in the media, and in common behavior.

## NOT ALLOWING OURSELVES TO BE MARGINALIZED

Christians must not resign themselves to becoming marginal, left in the lurch by the dominant culture. We must realize that our central values have been gradually eroded. Consider, for example, some of the taboo words in our cultural milieu: *virtue, grace, penance, interior life, conversion, silence, contemplation, cross, resurrection, life in the Spirit, the imitation of Christ.* If our contemporaries no longer understand the words that express our hope, then how can we attract them to Jesus Christ? The young, especially, are profoundly influenced by the spirit of the times and its radical devaluation of religion. Youth are both the witnesses and the victims of the religious crisis. But they are also, and even more, the revealers of contemporary aspirations. It is through them alone that we will really be able to create a new culture of hope.[6]

## AN ANTHROPOLOGY OPEN TO THE SPIRIT

To evangelize cultures, we need an anthropological approach to pastoral ministry. The social sciences can render valuable service when it comes to cultural discernment and analysis. The main advantage of modern anthropology is its definition of the human being in terms of culture, that is, in the psycho-social context in which people reveal themselves. John Paul II has insisted a number of times on this approach in evangelization. "The human being becomes the path of the Church in ever new ways."[7] The perception of the human as a being of reason and freedom is greatly enriched by the modern anthropological view of human reality as culture. John Paul II has put it this way: "Recent progress in cultural and philosophical anthropology shows that one cannot obtain a more precise definition of human reality than in terms of culture. This definition characterizes human beings as such and distinguishes them from other beings, as clearly as does reason, freedom, or language."[8]

Reaching persons in the midst of their cultural milieu enables the evangelizer to discover the harsh conditioning that so many people undergo and to grasp their sense of spiritual agony. If we only look more carefully, we can see that this spiritual anguish is often a preparation for the discovery of salvation in Jesus Christ. Paul Tillich describes this experience of human fragility as a predisposition to faith:

> Only those who have experienced the shock of transitoriness, anxiety in which they are aware of their finitude, the threat of nonbeing, can understand what the notion of God means. Only those who have experienced the tragic ambiguities of our historical existence and have totally questioned the meaning of existence can understand what the symbol of the Kingdom of God means.[9]

The process of being able to read signs of moral distress and becoming aware of the immense need for hope that secularized culture secretly reveals will open a new path to evangelization.

## FOR THE REDEMPTION OF CULTURES

Ultimately, evangelization places cultures before the mystery of Christ, who died and rose for the salvation of all human reality. A radical split is inevitable: "a stumbling block to Jews, and an absurdity to Gentiles," Saint Paul said. The dynamism of evangelization is realized only in the encounter with Jesus Christ. He is the sole mediator through whom the Kingdom of God comes. The evangelization of cultures, like that of persons, finds its efficacy only in the strength of the Spirit, in prayer, in the witness of faith, in participating in the mystery of the Cross and Redemption. It would be a vain temptation to wish to change cultures through a simple psycho-social or socio-political operation. Evangelization, especially in the dark night of faith — and in the spiritual night of cultures — presupposes a conversion to the mystery of the Cross. To suffer this purification and to hope in the mysterious but sure ways of the Spirit, is the lot of all evangelizers of all times. It is painful to live in the anguish of the new world dimly taking shape around us, but consolation shall not be denied those who announce Jesus Christ to the world.

Evangelizing cultures presupposes the long-suffering patience of those who must sow without reaping, or who indeed will never reap the fruits of their labors. This calls for trust in the slow infiltration of the word in cultural reality. The famous Dominican preacher Lacordaire expressed it well: "I have not, perhaps, converted anyone, that is true. But I have converted public opinion—that is, everyone."[10] Today as yesterday, evangelization is capable of creating culture, even when its invisible germination cannot be foreseeable or programmed. We will render a real service to evangelization if we learn to defend the *humanum* and its highest values, ever seeking to bring the response of Christ to the latent aspirations of all cultures.

## THE SIGNIFICANCE OF CHRISTIANIZING CULTURES

There is no doubt that the new evangelization is directed to persons as well as to cultures as such. Cultures must then be Christianized, that is, be converted to the ideals of the Gospel. This point needs clarification in order to avoid misconceptions about the mission of the Church that could be construed as the imposition of a "Christian social system."

Vatican II clearly reminded us that the Church has no cultural, social, or political order of her own to propose. Her mission is essentially religious. The Council, faithful to the constant thought of the Church, has said it once more: "Christ ... gave His Church no proper mission in the political, economic, or social order. The purpose which He set before her is a religious one. ... In virtue of her mission and nature she is bound to no particular form of human culture."[11] True, the word of Christ generates civilization, and the Gospel demands that faith become incarnate in cultures. But the Church imposes no single model of culture, no single plan for the earthly city. In the freedom of their social and cultural options, Christians cannot identify the Church with any one political platform or cultural policy. While it is indeed true that out of their Christian convictions they must commit themselves, they can never propose their social or political projects as those of the Church herself. The

role of the Church is of a different order. It consists in enlightening and purifying all cultures through the proclamation of
Gospel values and the promotion of human dignity. The Church
acknowledges a cultural mission, but it accomplishes it by proclaiming Jesus Christ, the source of truth, love, and justice. From
this source flow the principles capable of renewing all cultures
by calling them to transcend themselves. The first and most basic
cultural progress comes through the attention of human beings
to their spiritual calling. The proclamation of this truth by the
Church constitutes a form of in-depth cultural action whose
impact transforms all personal and social life. Thus, it is through
its faith in Jesus Christ that the Church seeks to serve culture
and cultures, continually calling them to the primacy of spiritual
and moral values. Christian faith, God's free gift to humanity,
transcends any given culture, and thus the Gospel has a universal capacity to regenerate all cultures.

We can indeed discover in every living culture traces of the
Spirit mysteriously operative in human history. We can admit as
well that a certain sense of the Absolute and the Sacred secretly
inspires every culture, and that there is no genuine culture without some religious foundation. This perspective could lend new
meaning to the dialogue with nonbelievers if we would learn
how to detect a commitment to absolute values and a subjective
sense of religion that underlies attitudes of "unbelief."

In the final analysis, to evangelize means to proclaim the
radical salvation of Jesus Christ, who purifies and elevates all
human reality, through the mystery of Death and Resurrection.
Cultures secretly yearn for hope and liberation. We have to
teach people how Jesus Christ brings a realization to this hope.
The answer of the Gospel is valid for individuals and cultures
alike, as John Paul II reminds us: "Since salvation is something
total and integral, it concerns the whole human being and all
human beings, and thus reaches the historical and social reality,
the culture, and the communitarian structures in which they
live."[12] Salvation cannot be reduced to earthly pursuits alone or
to the sole abilities of the human being. "Human beings are not
ultimately their own saviors. Salvation transcends the human
and the earthly. It is a gift from above. There is no self-redemption: God alone saves the human being, in Christ."[13]

## TRAINING FOR A PASTORAL MINISTRY TO CULTURE

The foregoing reflections lead us to formulate three practical suggestions as a preparation for the task of evangelizing cultures.

First, it is indispensable to acquire an ability for cultural analysis through study, reflection, and the practice of observation. Let us learn to discern new ways of thinking and behaving, the influence of the media, the impact of advertising and propaganda, and the values circulated by interest or pressure groups. The ability to assess cultural trends does not necessarily require special training in the social sciences. What is needed is a talent for empathy, that is, the concerned scrutiny of collective needs and hopes. Cultural analysis culminates in a new pastoral sensitivity and *evangelical discernment*.

This demands a shift from the geographical to a cultural view of evangelization. Paul VI formulated it for us in the most inspiring terms:

> For the Church it is a question not only of preaching the Gospel in ever wider geographic areas or to ever greater numbers of people, but also of affecting and as it were upsetting, through the power of the Gospel, mankind's criteria of judgment, determining values, points of interest, lines of thought, sources of inspiration and models of life, which are in contrast with the Word of God and the plan of salvation.[14]

Second, the evangelization of cultures calls for a new kind of concerted effort among all agents of pastoral ministry: priests, religious, laity, and all Catholic movements and organizations. The task is beyond the abilities of any one person. This concerted effort of evangelization, pursued in an ecumenical spirit, calls for special training in teamwork and a concerted strategy of evangelization. The Church has an urgent need for a *pastoral ministry to culture*. A collaborative effort is incumbent on all Christians to define the objectives of this ministry and the conditions required for its successful outcome.

There are encouraging signs that new programs for evangelizing cultures are developing in many parts of the Church. Some dioceses, like Rome itself, have appointed an Auxiliary Bishop for cultural activities; several Episcopal Conferences have created a special commission for faith and culture. Many cultural centers on various continents are actively engaged in the evangelization of culture, in inculturation, in cultural dialogue and development. Moreover, as previously explained in chapter 1, John Paul II, in 1982, founded the Pontifical Council for Culture, with the task of stimulating within the whole Church the commitment to evangelize the cultures of our age and to promote everywhere the cultural development of all men and women. All these efforts are concrete ways to implement the call of Vatican II for a new proclamation of the Gospel to the modern world. Still there is much to be done before the new evangelization will function fully and efficiently. Hopefully, the awareness is already there, as a promising sign for the future of evangelization in modern societies.[15]

Third, a *new language* is needed if we are to reach the mentalities of the present age. The central message that we are to communicate with persuasiveness is that the cultures and persons of today radically need to be redeemed in Jesus Christ. The mentalities of the present age often nourish the illusion that individuals can liberate themselves and find happiness by their own efforts. This is the deceptive utopia of self-redemption, which can only lead to disenchantment and despair. It is this spiritual shield that we must pierce with the power and gentleness of the Gospel. Jesus Christ alone can deliver and save; he alone is the answer to the enigma of the human condition wounded by sin and yearning for hope.

In sum, the conviction that inspires the work of evangelization is that each and every human person and culture has already been redeemed by Christ: the Good News still waits to be announced. This theological conviction is the main motivation that evangelizers must acquire in our day and age. In proclaiming the novelty of the Gospel, the Church becomes a creator of human culture. The Kingdom of God is subject to no limits. "God penetrates wherever he is allowed to enter," said Martin Buber.

The evangelizer can trust and take courage in the certitude

that God has enkindled in human hearts a thirst for the Infinite. Are Christians attuned enough to this spiritual hunger in men and women of today? Father de Lubac recalled the urgency and gravity of the question: "Man does not live by bread alone. The spirit does not wait, cannot wait. The soul's hunger is as brutal as that of the body. It is just as lethal. The only difference is that, while too little attention is paid to those who are suffering the starvation of the body, those suffering the soul's starvation attract no attention at all."[16]

The call to evangelize today's minds and cultures would seem an unbearable task if measured against a purely human yard-stick. Fortunately, after Vatican II, the Church has modernized her perception of cultures and has definitely committed herself to bring the message of Christ to the emerging civilization of our times.[17]

# References

## INTRODUCTION: EVANGELIZING THE CULTURE OF MODERNITY

1. See Cardinal Leo Jozef Suenens, "Spirit of Renewal," *The Tablet* (September 19, 1992), p. 1157.

2. John Paul II, *Centesimus Annus,* May 31, 1991, No. 51.

3. John Paul II, *Discourse to the International Council for Catechesis* (Coincat), September 26, 1992.

## 1. THE CHURCH'S PERCEPTION OF MODERNITY

1. John XXIII, Opening Speech to the Council (October 11, 1962); English translation in W. M. Abbott (ed.), *The Documents of Vatican II.* New York, 1966, pp. 712-716.

2. G. B. Cardinal Montini, *Discorsio al Clero 1957-1967.* Milan, 1963, pp. 78-80.

3. R. Aubert, "Attentes des Eglises et du monde au moment de l'élection de Paul VI," in *Ecclesiam Suam. Première Encyclique de Paul VI. Colloque International. Rome, 24-26 octobre 1980.* Brescia, 1982, pp. 11-39. Cited here: p. 17.

4. See *ibid.,* p. 20.

5. Paul VI, Opening Speech to the Second Session of the Council (September 29, 1963), in *Documenti: Il Concilio Vaticano II.* Rome, 1966, p. 1018.

6. K. Rahner, "Toward a Fundamental Theological Interpretation of Vatican II," *Theological Studies* 40 (1979), pp. 716-727, cited here: p. 723.

7. A. Dupront, "Le Concile de Trente," in *Le Concile et les Conciles, Contribution à l'histoire de la vie conciliaire de l'Eglise.* Paris, 1960, pp. 195-243.

8. See R. Aubert, M. Gueret, and P. Tombeur, *Concilium Vaticanum I. Concordances, Index, Listes de fréquence, Tables comparatives.*

Louvain, 1977, pp. 202-240. (Comparisons between the vocabulary of Vatican I and that of Vatican II.)

9. Rev. Corson, quoted in Aubert, "Attentes des Eglises et du monde au moment de l'élection de Paul VI," p. 39.

10. Paul VI, Opening Speech to the Third Session of the Council (September 14, 1964), in *Documenti: Il Concilio Vaticano II,* p. 1037.

11. G.-M. Cardinal Garrone, *Cinquante ans de vie d'Église, la voix d'un grand témoin.* Paris, 1984, p. 27.

12. Dupront, "Le Concile de Trente," pp. 242-243, observed, for example, that the Council of Trent had practically paid no attention to the social problems of the emerging world of its times: "Another more basic characteristic of the temporal Tridentine world: the body of Tridentine decrees remained silent on the invasive rise of modern capitalism, especially as to the moral problems posed by commerce and the money trade, while Calvinism tried gropingly to address them. The whole world of prelates and clergy of Trent were convinced that the scholastic teaching sufficed on the matter. Yet Trent was an important stop on the trade route of precious metals from India to the Empire. Were they blind to their times? History cannot but pose the question in pursuit of a deeper understanding."

13. This is very marked, for example, in the two discourses of Pius XII concerning "Christian civilization," September 1, 1944, and February 29, 1946.

14. The "social" schemata of Vatican I were well analyzed in the thesis published at the Gregorian University by Paolo Petruzzi, *Chiesa e società civile al Concilio Vaticano I.* Rome, 1984.

15. It is interesting to note the parallels between the definition of culture found in *Gaudium et Spes* 53 and that adopted by UNESCO in Mexico in 1983, at the World Conference on Cultural Policies. The UNESCO definition is found in *Mondiacult: Bilan d'une Conference, Presence Catholique.* Paris, 1982, pp. 3-4; the following English translation is found in *Church and Cultures,* 1 (1984), 13.

"Culture may now be said to be the whole complex distinctive, spiritual, material, intellectual and emotional features that characterize a society or social group. It includes not only the arts and letters, but also modes of life, the fundamental rights of human beings, value systems, traditions and beliefs; it is culture that gives man the ability to reflect upon himself. It is culture that makes us specifically human, rational beings, endowed with a critical judgment and a sense of moral commitment. It is through culture that we discern values and make choices. It is through culture that man expresses himself, becomes aware of himself, recognizes his incompleteness, questions his own achievements, seeks untiringly for new meanings and creates works through which he transcends his limitations."

16. Paul VI, Closing Speech to the Council (December 7, 1965), in *Documenti: Il Concilio Vaticano II*, p. 1080.

17. See the testimony of P. Charles, in *Etudes Missiologiques*. Louvain, 1956, p. 137.

18. See the Message of the 1977 Synod to the People of God, in *L'Osservatore Romano* (English edition) (November 3, 1977), p. 3.

19. Paul VI, Apostolic Exhortation *Evangelii Nuntiandi* (1975), 20; English translation, in Australian Edition, St. Paul Publications, 1982, p. 25.

20. John Paul II, Letter Instituting the Pontifical Council for Culture, in *AAS* 74 (1983), pp. 683-688; English translation in *L'Osservatore Romano* (June 28, 1982). The Pontifical Council for Culture was restructured and given wider responsiblities by the "Motu Proprio" of John Paul II, of March 25, 1993, cf. *L'Osservatore Romano* (May 5, 1993).

## 2. MODERNITY AS A CULTURE TO EVANGELIZE

1. Autograph Letter for the foundation of the Pontifical Council for Culture, May 20, 1982, *A.A.S.* 74 (1983), 683-688.

2. John Paul II to the Pontifical Council for Culture, January 15, 1985.

3. *Gaudium et Spes*, Nos. 4-10. The working definition of *culture* we are adopting is the one used by *Gaudium et Spes*, No. 53. I have discussed the modern relevance of that definition in my book *Gospel Message and Human Cultures: From Leo XIII to John Paul II*. Pittsburgh, PA, Duquesne University Press, 1989, chs. 1 and 2.

4. For a review of current methods in cultural analysis, see R. Wuthnow, *Meanings and Moral Order: Exploration in Cultural Analysis*. Berkeley, University of California Press, 1987. See H. Carrier, *Lexique de la Culture. Pour l'Analyse culturelle et l'Inculturation*. Paris, Desclée, 1992.

5. Paul Cardinal Poupard (ed.), *Galileo Galilei: Toward a Resolution of 350 Years of Debate, 1633-1983*. Pittsburgh, PA, Duquesne University Press, 1987; see chapter 5, n. 22.

6. Lewis Mumford, *The Culture of Cities*. New York, Harcourt, Brace and Co., 1938, p. 3.

7. K. Marx, *A Contribution to the Critique of Political Economy* (First published in Berlin, 1859).

8. This ethical and cultural approach to development is firmly

stressed in the encyclical of John Paul II, *Sollicitudo Rei Socialis*, December 30, 1987. An analogous approach is adopted by the "World Decade of Cultural Development" decided by the United Nations for 1988-1997.

9. D. J. de S. Price, *Science since Babylon*. New Haven, Yale University, 1962, p. 107.

10. M. Ginsberg, *The Idea of Progress: A Reevaluation*. London, Methuen, 1953, p. 53; and by the same author, *On Justice in Society*. Baltimore, MD, Penguin Books, 1965.

11. W. W. Rostow, *The Stages of Economic Growth*. New York, 1960.

12. Address to the 26th Congress of the Communist Party, Moscow, March 1981. Even Mikhail Gorbachev had felt obliged in his first speeches to proclaim the traditional socialist utopia based on "the Leninian interpretation . . . of an inexorable movement forward" (Speech to the Plenum of April 1985).

13. T. Adorno, *Dialectique négative*. Paris, Payot, 1978, p. 250.

14. These values are well described in several documents of Vatican II: religious freedom and commitment, *Dignitatis Humanae*, 3, 10; critical attitude and purification of faith, *Gaudium et Spes*, 7; active participation in liturgy, *Sacrosanctum Concilium*, 14; the use of research and social sciences, *Christus Dominus*, 16, 17; initiative and commitment of lay people, *Lumen Gentium*, 37; freedom of research and expression, *Gaudium et Spes*, 62.

15. Henri Bergson analyzed with great insight this native sociability and human need for intimate communities, even in complex societies: "Originally and basically, the moral structure of man was made for simple and delimited societies. No matter how civilized humanity may become, no matter what transformations society may undergo, we maintain that tendencies which are, so to speak, an organic part of social existence, have remained what they were at the beginning. We can rediscover and observe them" (Henri Bergson, *Les deux sources de la morale et de la religion*. Paris, Alcan, 1934, 16th Edition, p. 53).

16. A. W. Gouldner, *The Future of Intellectuals and the Rise of the New Class*. New York, Seabury Press, 1979, p. 59.

17. Mircea Eliade, *Le sacré et le profane*. Paris, Gallimard, 1965, p. 172.

18. Those are conclusions of studies conducted by M.I.T. in the USA; see Norman Myers, *The GAIA Atlas of Planet Management*. New York, London, Pan Books, 1985.

19. Cf. Lévi-Strauss, *La pensée sauvage*. Paris, Plon, 1962, p. 236.

20. Paul Ricoeur, "La Philosophie," in *Tendances principales de la recherche dans les sciences sociales et humaines*. Paris, Mouton/Unesco,

1978, 2nd Part, Volume II, pp. 1127-1645, citation p. 1539.

21. Kenneth Boulding, "The Emerging Superculture," in K. Baier and N. Rescher (ed.), *Values and the Future*. London, Macmillan, 1969, pp. 336-350, cf. p. 347; quoted in G. Claeys, see note 23.

22. H. Arendt, "Dream and Nightmare," *Commonweal*, Sept. 10, 1954, p. 610; quoted in G. Claeys, see note 23.

23. Gregory Claeys, "Culture de masse et culture universelle: américanisation et protectionisme culturel," in *Diogène* 136 (Oct.-Dec. 1986), pp. 76-102.

24. Mircea Eliade, *Fragments d'un journal*. Paris, Gallimard, 1973, pp. 179-180.

25. This aspect of inculturation is discussed in Chapter 3. See also Louis Luzbetak, *The Church and Cultures: New Perspectives in Missiological Anthropology*. Maryknoll, N.Y., Orbis Books, 1988, and H. Carrier, *Gospel Message and Human Cultures*, quoted in footnote 3.

26. In the proposition condemned by the *Syllabus*, all the elements are interrelated: "Romanus Pontifex potest ac debet cum progressu, cum liberalismo et cum recenti civilitate sese reconciliare et componere" ("The Roman Pontiff can and must reconcile himself and compromise with progress, liberalism and modern civilization") Pius IX, *Syllabus*, 1864, No. 80, *Denzinger-Schönmetzer*, 2980.

27. This normative principle of inculturation is studied more at length in Chapter 3.

28. Henri-Irénée Marrou, *Crise de notre temps et réflexion chrétienne (de 1930 à 1975)*. Paris, Editions Beauchesne, 1978; see "Une civilisation d'inspiration chrétienne", pp. 41-53: cit. pp. 50-51; see his classic study *Saint Augustin et la fin de la culture antique*, Paris, 1958, 4th ed.; and also his essay *St. Augustine and His Influence through the Ages*. London, 1957. Vatican II used several times the image of the Christians as "the soul of human society": see *Gaudium et Spes*, No. 40; *Lumen Gentium*, No. 38, which quotes *Epist. ad Diognetum*, No. 6, referred to by Marrou.

29. Autograph Letter for the foundation of the Pontifical Council for Culture, May 20, 1982, *A.A.S.* 74 (1983), 683-688.

30. John Paul II to the Pontifical Council for Culture, January 18, 1983.

### 3. INCULTURATION: A MODERN APPROACH TO EVANGELIZATION

1. The main source of documentation for this chapter is taken from: Hervé Carrier, *Gospel Message and Human Cultures: From Leo XIII to*

*John Paul II.* Translated from the French by John Drury. Pittsburgh, PA, Duquesne University Press, 1989.

2. Let us recall in particular: Benedict XV, *Maximum Illud* (1919); Pius XI, *Rerum Ecclesiae* (1926); Pius XII, *Evangelii Praecones* (1951); John Paul II, *Redemptoris Missio* (1990). Other documents of Paul VI and John Paul II concerning the missions will be considered later on.

3. The first citation is from *Evangelii Praecones* (1951) of Pius XII; the other one is from his first encyclical, *Summi Pontificatus* (1939).

4. See the document, "Faith and Inculturation," prepared by the International Theological Commission in collaboration with the Pontifical Council for Culture in *Origins,* May 1989, pp. 800-807.

5. John Paul II offers a brief definition of inculturation that well describes the idea of reciprocity: "Inculturation is the incarnation of the Gospel message in autochthonous cultures and, at the same time, the introduction of those cultures into the life of the Church": from his encyclical letter *Slavorum Apostoli* (June 2, 1986), for the eleventh centenary of Saints Cyril and Methodius. The document is important for an exploration of the meaning of inculturation and the evangelization of cultures from a historical viewpoint.

6. In 1936 Robert Redfield and two colleagues offered an epochmaking definition of acculturation to their fellow anthropologists: "Acculturation comprehends those phenomena which result when groups of individuals having different cultures come into continuous first contact, with subsequent changes in the original cultural patterns of either or both groups" (Robert Redfield, Ralph Linton, and Melville J. Herskovits, "Outline for the Study of Acculturation," *American Anthropologist* 38 [1936], pp. 149-152). This was a memorandum prepared by the three anthropologists at the request of the Social Research Council, which had asked them to draw a clearer picture of the growing field of studies dealing with "acculturation."

7. John Paul II to the Biblical Commission, April 26, 1979; to the bishops of Kenya, May 7, 1980; see also the encyclical *Slavorum Apostoli* (June 2, 1986); cf. address to the University of Coimbra, May 15, 1982.

8. John Paul II, to the Pontifical Council for Culture, January 18, 1983.

9. Paul VI, *Evangelii Nuntiandi* (1975), No. 20.

10. John Paul II stressed the evangelizing capacity of the *family* in his address to the Nigerian bishops in Lagos: "It is above all when the Christian families have been truly evangelized and are aware of their evangelizing role that there can be an effective *evangelization of culture*—an effective encounter between the Gospel and culture" (February 15, 1982). On this subject see also the apostolic exhortations

*Familiaris Consortio* (November 22, 1981), Nos. 42-54; *Christifideles Laici* (December 30, 1988), No. 40.

11. John Paul II, to the Pontifical Council for Culture, January 15, 1985.

12. John Paul II, Letter of foundation of the Pontifical Council for Culture, May 20, 1982, *AAS* 74 (1983), pp. 683-688.

13. Pius XI, to Rev. M. D. Roland-Gosselin, *Semaines sociales de France.* Versailles, 1936, pp. 416-462. Cited in *Gaudium et Spes,* No. 58.

14. Paul VI, *Evangelii Nuntiandi,* No. 19.

15. Declaration of the Secretariat for Non-Christians, *Attitudes of the Catholic Church Toward Believers of Other Religions,* Pentecost 1984, *AAS* 76 (1984), pp. 816-828; see also *Dialogue and Proclamation.* Reflections and Orientations on the Interreligious Dialogue and Proclamation of the Gospel of Jesus-Christ. Published by the Congregation for the Evangelization of Peoples and the Pontifical Council for Interreligious Dialogue, Vatican City, May 19, 1993, Nos. 42-46.

16. John Paul II has given a testimony of this spiritual attitude in the memorable meeting of prayer held in Assisi, October 27, 1986, with religious leaders of the world. About the Muslims, in particular, John Paul II said to the new Ambassador of Nigeria to the Holy See: "As you know, the Church has a deep respect for Muslims, since she believes that the plan of salvation encompasses all who acknowledge the Creator. This respect includes a readiness to cooperate with them for the betterment of humanity, and a commitment to search together for true peace and justice" (*L'Osservatore Romano,* October 28, 1988).

17. John Paul II, *Sollicitudo Rei Socialis* (December 30, 1987); *Centesimus Annus* (May 1, 1991); words quoted are from this last encyclical, No. 5; see also Nos. 51, 54.

18. John Paul II, to the Pontifical Council for Culture, January 15, 1985.

19. John Paul II explained the transcendence of God's word over every culture: "Evangelization aims at penetrating and elevating culture by the power of the Gospel. On the other hand, we know that God's *revelation exceeds the insights of any culture and of all the cultures of the world put together*" (to the bishops of Nigeria, February 15, 1982).

20. 1 Cor. 1:22-23.

21. John XXIII, encyclical *Princeps Pastorum* (November 28, 1959), No. 17.

22. This is not meant to minimize the historical role of European Christianity as it developed over the centuries. John Paul II, speaking to the Council of Europe, in Strasbourg, October 1988, recalled the

fundamental contribution of that continent: "In almost twenty centuries, Christianity has contributed in building a *conception of the world and of man* which remains fundamental, beyond all the divisions, weaknesses, even the abandonments of Christians themselves. . . . During centuries, Europe played a considerable role in the other parts of the world. We have to admit that Europe has not always done its best in the encounter with other civilizations, but no one can deny that it has fortunately been able to share many of the values it had slowly developed. The sons of Europe had an essential part in the diffusion of the Christian message" (October 8, 1988). In *Catechesi Tradendae* (1979), the Pope shows the link between the Gospel message and the historical contexts in which it was inserted: "The Gospel message cannot be purely and simply isolated from the culture in which it was first inserted (the biblical world or, more concretely, the cultural milieu in which Jesus of Nazareth lived), nor, without serious loss, from the cultures in which it has already been expressed down the centuries" (No. 53).

23. John Paul II, to the Biblical Commission, April 26, 1979. Addressing the Kenyan bishops (May 5, 1980), the Pope declared: "The 'acculturation' or 'inculturation' which you rightly promote will truly be a reflection of the Incarnation of the Word, when a culture, transformed and regenerated by the Gospel, brings forth from its own living tradition original expressions of Christian life, celebration and thought" (cf. *Catechesi Tradendae, 53*). See also note 7 above.

24. *Evangelii Nuntiandi,* No. 20.

25. John Paul II, address to the University of Coimbra, Portugal, May 15, 1982. The Pope developed the same idea in his speech to the bishops of Nigeria (February 15, 1982), explaining how the "cultural incarnation" continues through history: "It is through the providence of God that the divine message is made incarnate and is communicated through the culture of each people. It is for ever true that the *path of culture is the path of man,* and it is on this path that man encounters the One who embodies the values of all cultures and fully reveals the man of each culture to himself. The Gospel of Christ the Incarnate Word finds its home along the path of culture and from this path it continues to offer its message of salvation and eternal life." See also *Catechesi Tradendae,* No. 53, and note 22 above.

26. Vatican II, *Lumen Gentium,* No. 13.

27. John Paul II, to the Roman Curia, December 22, 1984.

28. *L'Osservatore Romano,* May 1, 1977.

29. Paul VI, Address to the symposium of the Episcopal Conferences of Africa and Madagascar, September 26, 1975.

30. Paul VI, to the bishops of Asia, November 28, 1970.

31. John Paul II, Address to the Roman Curia, December 22, 1984.

32. Final Report of the extraordinary Synod of bishops of 1985, *L'Osservatore Romano* (Engl.), December 16, 1985.

33. Vatican II, *Ad Gentes*, No. 22.

34. *Ibid.*, No. 11.

35. Vatican II, *Sacrosanctum Concilium*, No. 37.

36. Quoted by Paul VI, *Evangelii Nuntiandi*, No. 53.

37. *Ad Gentes*, No. 22.

38. *Evangelii Nuntiandi*, No. 63.

39. In particular, African traditional religion (ATR) rightly deserves greater pastoral attention and a study program has been proposed to the Episcopal Conferences and to the whole Church in Africa: see Cardinal Francis Arinze, *Pastoral Attention to African Traditional Religion*: Letter of the President of the Secretariat for non-Christians to the Presidents of all Episcopal Conferences in Africa and Madagascar. March 25, 1988; section 16 of that document reads: "In each country or cultural area it will be useful to study and document what efforts have already been made by the Church to meet the prevailing ATR and culture, and with what results. In this exercise it is helpful to take the major elements of ATR and ask how Christianity has met each of them, and also to examine ideas which are entirely new to ATR and which Christianity should emphasize." See *African Ecclesial Review* 30 (June 1988), pp. 131-134.

40. Besides the African experience of inculturation, there is also the typical inculturation which took place in China, in India, in Latin America: see H. Carrier, *Gospel Message and Human Cultures*, Chapter 8, and H. Carrier, *Evangelio y Culturas: De Leon XIII a Juan Pablo II*. Bogota, CELAM, 1991, Chps. 10-14.

41. Paul VI, to the bishops of Africa and Madagascar, assembled in Kampala, July 31, 1969.

42. Paul VI, Message to Africa, *Africae Terrarum*, October 29, 1967.

43. Declaration of the bishops of Africa and Madagascar present at the fourth Synod of Bishops, October 20, 1974.

44. Paul VI, at the canonization of the Martyrs of Uganda, October 18, 1964.

45. The ecumenical dialogue is usually a slow process, but practical cooperation is more readily possible, as Vatican II noted: "Catholics should collaborate with their separate brothers, following the dispositions of the decree on ecumenism, cooperating in social, technical, cultural and religious matters . . ." *Ad Gentes*, No. 15; cf. *Unitatis Redintegratio*, Nos. 4 and 9. All Christian Churches face the serious problems of sects and new religious movements. The Holy See has published on

the subject the result of a survey among all Episcopal Conferences, conducted by the Secretariats for Christian Unity, for non-Christian religions, for non-Believers and the Pontifical Council for Culture. See *Sects or New Religious Movements: Pastoral Challenge.* Rome, May 3, 1986.

46. Paul VI, *Africae Terrarum* (1967).

47. Paul VI, address of September 26, 1975.

48. Paul VI, to the bishops of Africa, October 28, 1977.

49. Paul VI, Message of the Church to the Peoples of Africa, August 1, 1969.

50. John Paul II, to the bishops of Zaire, Kinshasa, May 3, 1980.

51. *Ibid.*

52. John Paul II, meeting with representatives of the cultural world, Yaoundé, August 13, 1985.

53. John Paul II, address to priests, religious, and committed lay persons, Kinshasa, August 15, 1985.

54. John Paul II, homily in Bangui, August 14, 1985.

55. John Paul II, to the laity, in Kadura, Nigeria, February 14, 1982.

56. John Paul II, to the bishops of Nigeria, in visit "ad limina," *L'Osservatore Romano* (Engl.), September 14, 1987; see also note 39 above.

57. John Paul II, homily in Lomé, August 8, 1985.

58. John Paul II, address to the Cameroon Episcopal Conference, August 13, 1985.

59. John Paul II, address to civil authorities and the Diplomatic Corps, Kinshasa, August 15, 1985.

60. John Paul II, meeting with representatives of the cultural world, Yaoundé, August 13, 1986. The expression recurs frequently during his visit in August 1985.

61. John Paul II, to the bishops of Kenya, May 5, 1980.

62. John Paul II, *Sollicitudo Rei Socialis* (1987), No. 30.

63. *Ibid.,* No. 31.

64. Problems concerning evangelization and modernity have been studied by the International Theological Commission and the Pontifical Council for Culture in the document "Faith and Inculturation" quoted in note 4 above. See Chapters 1 and 2.

65. *Ad Gentes,* No. 22.

66. John Paul II, 6th apostolic visit to Africa, Jan. 25-Feb. 1, 1990.

67. John Paul II, Encyclical *Redemptoris Missio* on the Missions (December 7, 1990), Nos. 52-54.

68. John Paul II to the Pontifical Council for Culture, January 17, 1987.

## 5. TOWARD A NEW CONVERGENCE OF SCIENCE
## AND RELIGION

1. Aristotle, *Nicomachean Ethics* VI, 3.

2. *Méditations métaphysiques: Réponse aux Deuxièmes Objections, I.*

3. Voltaire wrote abundantly on Newton, in particular his book *Eléments de la philosophie de Newton.* Lausanne, 1772 (new ed.); Voltaire's letters refer more than 100 times to Newton: cf. *Correspondance.* Paris, Gallimard, 1963.

4. Jean Rostand. *The Substance of Man.* New York, Doubleday, 1962, p. 15.

5. C. Lévi-Strauss. *The Savage Mind.* Chicago, University of Chicago Press, 1966, p. 247.

6. Thomas B. Macauley, *Minute on Indian Education*, reprinted in *Prose and Poetry.* Cambridge, MA, Harvard University Press, 1952.

7. These studies have been well assessed by Cantore and Holton, whose publications I found helpful on the subject. See, in particular, Enrico Cantore, *Scientific Man: The Humanistic Significance of Science.* New York, Institute for Scientific Humanism, 1977; and Gerald Holton, *The Scientific Imagination: Case Studies.* New York, Cambridge University Press, 1979; cf. also G. Holton's essay indicated below, note 17.

8. See the discussion on the subject in G. Holton (1977), pp. 268-274.

9. *Opticks* Q. 31.

10. F. Herneck. "Albert Einsteins gesprochenes Glaubensbekenntnis," *Die Naturwissenschaften* 53 (1966), p. 198.

11. H. Poincaré, *Science and Method.* New York, Dover, p. 22.

12. Quoted in E. Cantore (1977), p. 97.

13. M. Planck, *Scientific Autobiography and Other Papers.* New York, Philosophical Library, 1949, p. 120.

14. A. Einstein, *Ideas and Opinions.* New York, Crown, 1954, p. 40.

15. The religious attitude of Einstein is not easily described in a word. If he professed to be an agnostic, he also declared in a letter: "I am a deeply religious unbeliever." He explained in what sense he was religious: "To perceive that, behind what can be experienced, something is hidden which is unattainable for our spirit — something whose beauty and sublimity reach us only indirectly and by way of a pale reflection — this is religiousness. In this sense I am religious. It is enough for me to sense these mysteries with astonishment and to attempt, in humility, to formulate with my mind a scanty representation of the sublime structure of reality" (F. Herneck, *op. cit.*, p. 198).

16. B. Russell, *The Scientific Outlook*. New York, Norton, 1959, pp. 262-264.

17. G. Holton, "Sur les processus de l'invention scientifique durant les percées révolutionnaires" in Michel Cazenave (ed.), *Sciences et Symboles*. Colloque de Tsukuba. Paris, Albin Michel, 1986, pp. 53-75.

18. Cf. G. Holton (1986), p. 74.

19. *Science and the Boundaries of Knowledge: The Prologue of Our Cultural Past*. International Conference (Venice, 3-7 March 1986). (In French *La science face aux confins de la connaissance: le prologue de notre passé culturel*. Unesco-Giorgio Cini Foundation, Paris, UNESCO, 1987.

20. D. L. Lach, *Asia in the Making of Europe*. Chicago, University of Chicago Press, 1977, vol. II, p. 415.

21. See the discussions of John Eccles, H. Morowitz, F. Northrop, Henry Margenau, and several others. For instance, H. Margenau, Professor of Physics and Natural Philosophy at Yale University, has attempted a provocative synthesis of scientific and religious thought in *The Miracle of Existence*. Woodbridge, CT, Ox Bow Press, 1984.

22. See Report of the Galileo Commission and the Address of the Pope, on October 31, 1993, cf. *L'Osservatore Romano* (English), November 4, 1992.

23. For the Catholic Church, one can recall the work of the Pontifical Academy of Sciences, which has celebrated its 50th anniversary in 1986. It is opened to renowned scientists of all creeds and opinions. An interesting study on "Science and Islam" was presented at the Venice conference (see note 19 above) by Prof. Abdus Salam, Nobel Prize winner, Director of the International Center of Theoretical Physics, Trieste.

24. John Paul II, Message to Rev. George V. Coyne, S.J., Director of the Vatican Observatory, June 1, 1988, quoted in R. J. Russell, W. R. Stoeger, S.J., G. V. Coyne, S.J. (eds.), *Physics, Philosophy and Theology: A Common Quest for Understanding*. Notre Dame, IN, University of Notre Dame Press, 1988.

25. *Ibid.*

## 6. CHRISTIANS AND THE MODERN CONCEPTION OF CULTURAL RIGHTS

1. Those of the first generation are the civil and political rights; those of the second, the economic and social rights; those of the third generation refer to a right to solidarity, to a communal human right, and to the rights of the community.

2. Further bibliographical information on this theme is as follows: H. Carrier, *Lexique de la culture.* Tournai/Louvain-la Neuve, Desclée, 1992. See entries: "Biens culturels, Droits culturels, Politique culturelle"; G. Filibeck, ed., *The Right to Development. Conciliar and Pontifical Texts (1960-1990).* Pontifical Council for Justice and Peace, Vatican City, 1991; J. M. Pontier, J. C. Ricci, and J. Bourdon, *Droit de la culture.* Paris, Dalloz, 1990; M. Verwilghen, ed., *Droits de l'homme. Recueil de documents nationaux et internationaux.* Brussels, Louvain, Bruylant-AEDI, 1989; *Diritti economici, sociali e culturali nella prospettiva di un nuove Stato sociate.* Padua, 1990, No. 5.

3. H. Carrier, *Gospel Message and Human Cultures.* Pittsburgh, PA, Duquesne University Press, 1987. See Ch. 5, "Governments and Their Cultural Policies," pp. 57-71.

4. See H. Carrier, *Gospel Message and Human Cultures,* pp. 60-66.

5. John Paul II, *Centesimus Annus* (May 1, 1991), No. 32.

6. Discourse for the 25th Anniversary of the Universal Declaration on Human Rights, December 10, 1973.

7. John Paul II, *Centesimus Annus* (May 1, 1991), No. 51.

8. John Paul II, Encyclical *Sollicitudo Rei Socialis* (December 30, 1987), No. 33.

9. See *Journal of Legal Pluralism,* "Special issue on French Legal Anthropology," 29, 1990; Etienne LeRoy, "Les Fondements anthropologiques des droits de l'homme: Crise de l'universalisme et postmodernité," in *La Revue de Droit Prospectif,* XVII:48 (1992), pp. 131-160; Norbert Rouland, *Anthropologie Juridique.* Paris, P.U.F., 1988.

## 7. THE NEW EVANGELIZATION FACING AGNOSTIC CULTURE

1. One of the strongest statements on the evangelization of cultures is found in Paul VI, *Evangelii Nuntiandi* (1975): "The split between the Gospel and culture is without a doubt the drama of our time, just as it was of other times. Therefore every effort must be made to ensure a full evangelization of culture, or more correctly of cultures. They have to be regenerated by an encounter with the Gospel. But this encounter will not take place if the Gospel is not proclaimed" (No. 20).

2. John Paul II, Address to the Pontifical Council for Culture, January 15, 1985.

3. Bossuet, *Pensées détachées,* II.

4. John Paul II, at Santiago de Compostela, Spain, November 9, 1982, No. 6.

5. T. Parsons, "The Problem of Secularization," *Social Research* 41 (1974), pp. 493-525.

6. H. Carrier, *Cultures: notre avenir.* Rome, Gregorian University Press, 1985, Ch. III: "Les jeunes et la culture qui s'annonce."

7. John Paul II, *Encyclical on the Holy Spirit* (1986), No. 58.

8. John Paul II, Address at the University of Coimbra, Portugal, May 15, 1982.

9. Paul Tillich, *Systematic Theology.* Chicago, University of Chicago Press, 1951, Vol. I, pp. 61-62.

10. Cited by J. Loew, *Journal d'une mission ouvrière.* Paris, Cerf, 1963, p. 238.

11. *Gaudium et Spes,* No. 42. The same document (No. 58) quotes this text of Pius XI: "It is necessary never to lose sight of the fact that the objective of the Church is to evangelize, not to civilize. If it civilizes, it is through evangelization" (1936). It further quotes (No. 42) these words of Pius XII: "Its divine Founder, Jesus Christ, has not given it any mandate or fixed any end of the cultural order. The goal which Christ assigns to it is strictly religious. . . . The Church must lead men to God, in order that they may be given over to him without reserve. . . . The Church can never lose sight of the strictly religious, supernatural goal" (March 9, 1956).

12. John Paul II, Address to the Congress of Missiology, Urbanian University, Rome, *L'Osservatore Romano,* October 8, 1988.

13. *Ibid.*

14. Paul VI, *Evangelii Nuntiandi* (1975), No. 19.

15. The progress of this new pastoral approach is well illustrated in the following: Cardinal James Hickey, "The role of the Catholic university in the Church's mission of re-evangelization," *Communio* 19 (Summer 1992), pp. 254-270; Avery Dulles, "John Paul II and the New Evangelization," *America,* February 1, 1992, pp. 52 ff.

16. Henri de Lubac, *Nouveaux paradoxes.* Paris, 1955, p. 65.

17. H. Carrier, *Gospel Message and Human Cultures. From Leo XIII to John Paul II.* Pittsburgh, PA, Duquesne University Press, 1989.

# Index